PLANTS AND PLANTING PLANS
for a
BEE GARDEN

PLANTS AND PLANTING PLANS
for a
BEE GARDEN

How to design
beautiful borders that will attract bees

Maureen Little

SPRING HILL

For Georg

Published by Spring Hill, an imprint of How To Books Ltd.
Spring Hill House, Spring Hill Road
Begbroke, Oxford OX5 1RX
United Kingdom
Tel: (01865) 375794
Fax: (01865) 379162
info@howtobooks.co.uk
www.howtobooks.co.uk

First published 2012

How To Books greatly reduce the carbon footprint of their books
by sourcing their typesetting and printing in the UK.

British Library Cataloguing in Publication Data
A catalogue record of this book is available from the British Library.

ISBN: 978 1 905862 90 1

Produced for How To Books by Deer Park Productions, Tavistock, Devon
Designed and typeset by Mousemat Design Ltd
Printed and bound in Great Britain by Bell & Bain Ltd, Glasgow

NOTE: The material contained in this book is set out in good faith for general guidance and
no liability can be accepted for loss or expense incurred as a result of relying in particular cir-
cumstances on statements made in the book. Laws and regulations are complex and liable to
change, and readers should check the current position with relevant authorities before making
personal arrangements.

Contents

Acknowledgements

Generous relatives, friends and colleagues have encouraged and inspired me to write this book. I am indebted to all of them (and any mistakes you may find are entirely mine):

My friend and bee mentor, Toady, who introduced me to his beloved bees. He and they will always have a particular place in my life.

Giles Lewis and Nikki Read of Spring Hill Publishing – I always marvel at their faith in me.

And, most importantly, my family – Georg, Becca and James (and, of course, Susie). How could the garden of my life be so well designed and full of beautiful flowers, if not for them?

I would also like to say thank you to Tricia Brown of the Garden Studio, who enables me to keep my hand in – often in the soil, literally! – and who allowed me to take photographs of her plants; and to John Everiss of Bezza Nurseries, who allowed me to take photographs of his superb RHS Gold Medal garden, some of which are included in this book.

Introduction

*Have nothing in your house
that you do not know to be useful
or believe to be beautiful.*

This was the advice of William Morris, the influential craftsman, writer and social reformer of the 19th century, who is probably best remembered nowadays for his organic, garden-inspired designs for interior furnishing. You may wonder why I have chosen this quotation about interior design to begin a book about garden design and, more specifically, about plants and planting plans for a bee garden. Well, let's adjust the quotation slightly, so that it reads:

*Have no plant in your garden
that you do not know to be useful to bees
or believe to be beautiful.*

This now captures the essence, I think, of what I am trying to achieve here.

It probably goes without saying – but I make no apology for saying it again – that bees are vital to our planet's ecology and economy, and to our own well-being. The bad news is that without the pollinating services of bees of all kinds, our food supply would be severely compromised. The good news is that we can all do something to help. If each of us grew just a handful of bee-friendly plants in our gardens, this would provide an enormous resource for our buzzy friends – in fact, the phrase 'Think globally, act locally' could have been invented for bee-friendly gardeners!

So, what I would like to see in *every* garden are plants and flowers which are helpful to bees and which, at the same time, we find beautiful to look at.

It is, of course, the plants in a garden that are of paramount importance if we want to design a garden for bees. Many people think that in order to provide a suitable habitat for bees they have to plant a wild flower meadow or allow their garden to 'go native', eschewing their beloved garden plants. Certainly, bees adore wild and native flowers, but they also delight in a whole range of cultivated garden plants that are readily available at garden centres and nurseries.

Flowers provide bees with the food they need to survive, so this book will deal predominantly with questions like which plants are best for bees, and how we can arrange them together in suitable groupings that are attractive to bees as well as aesthetically pleasing to us. The plants that I have selected are just that – a selection – and are by no means the only ones that support bees. My choice of plants is subjective: I have chosen plants that are, from my experience and research, good for bees; but they are also ones that I personally like. I hope you will like my choice, too.

I have provided a range of garden plans later in the book. Rather than whole garden designs, with their accompanying hard landscaping and other features, you will find planting plans for different situations and of varying styles. I hope that you will be inspired enough by some of these planting ideas to try to transfer them to your own garden. You may find, of course, that you need to adapt the plans to suit your space; they are certainly not meant to be prescriptive, but to be ideas that aim to help you create your own 'bee border'. One whole garden design is included, however, which brings together some of the planting plans. This garden is a real one, and is, in fact, owned by a beekeeper.

You will notice that throughout the book I refer mostly (but not exclusively) to honeybees. There are two reasons for this. First, I help my friend, and bee mentor, Toady, look after his honeybees, so they have a special place in my heart. Second, and perhaps more importantly for this book, is that generally speaking, what is suitable in the way of flowers for honeybees is bound to be acceptable to both bumblebees and solitary bees, and indeed many other pollinating insects. (This is to do with the length of the bee's proboscis, which is generally shorter in honeybees than in other bees, so if a honeybee can reach the nectar, then other bees will be able to do so too.)

The first thing we will do in this book is assess the conditions in your garden – things like aspect and soil – that will affect how well (or otherwise) your plants will grow.

In Chapter 2 we give some thought to design 'tools' and how we can use them to create an attractive border. I also suggest a useful method of how we can arrange plants into groups, which will help us choose which ones to put together to make a good planting plan.

In Chapter 3 we look at 'bee-specific' things. We begin by examining very briefly some general factors that can make our garden as a whole more bee-friendly: things like providing water and suitable habitats for bumblebees and solitary bees – and, if you wish to keep honeybees for yourself, appropriate locations for beehives. We then focus on what makes a plant bee-friendly, and lastly look at which particular plant families are attractive to bees.

Chapter 4 is full of planting plans to give you some concrete ideas of how to put it all into practice.

Hardiness zone

My experience as a gardener is restricted to the British Isles, so all the recommendations I make and examples I give in this book are based on this. Our climate has been categorized as falling generally within hardiness zone 8a or 8b, so if you are gardening outside the British Isles, adjustments must be made.

Latin names of plants

I use Latin names of plants in all the planting plans. Where plant names appear in the text, I nearly always give the common name as well as the Latin one. The reason for doing this is that common names for plants can vary from region to region (a bluebell in Scotland is not the same as a bluebell in England, for example), so knowing the proper, undisputed Latin name is invaluable, especially when it comes to looking for plants in a nursery or online. The exceptions are vegetables; these are generally referred to by their common name. You will find an index of common names of plants and their Latin equivalents towards the end of the book.

Plant families

A word about the names of plant families. As a consequence of ongoing research, particularly with regard to DNA identification, reclassification of some plants has taken place. Some have been reclassified and put into different families, and some families have ceased to exist altogether. The latest reclassification, by the Angiosperm Phylogeny Group (APG), took place in 2009. However, in order to be as consistent as possible, I have used the family designation for each plant as found in *The Royal Horticultural Society Encyclopedia of Plants and Flowers*, 5th edition (see Further Reading).

1
Assessing the Conditions in Your Garden

Selecting bee-friendly plants and arranging them attractively in a border is only part of the process of creating a bee-friendly garden. We will look at plants and particular design aspects later in the book, but you first need to be aware of the existing conditions in your garden, including those over which you have little or no influence. I am thinking of things like the direction in which your border faces, the sort of soil you have, whether your garden is exposed or sheltered, and so on. These points may be mundane but they are nevertheless important – planting the right bee-friendly plant in the wrong place could prove both disappointing and expensive!

Aspect

The direction your planting area faces will have a significant bearing on what plants you can grow successfully. Most plants will survive in most situations, but you want your plants to thrive and be as strong and floriferous as possible to attract lots of bees. Generally speaking, most bee-friendly plants prefer a sunny aspect, which means that your garden should ideally face somewhere in the direction of south, or at least have sun for a good part of the day. In addition, research has shown that bees often ignore flowers growing in shady spots, even when they are ones that we know are attractive to them. So if you have a completely north-facing garden, the chances are that even if it contains bee-friendly plants, it will be overlooked in favour of a garden with flowers growing in the sun. This is not to say that it will be ignored altogether; there just won't be as many bees as in a sunny spot elsewhere.

Soil

There are many types of soil, ranging from clay to sand. Fortunately, few of us have soil that is only good for slapping on a potter's wheel, or is so sandy that nieces and nephews arrive with their buckets and spades. The majority of us have soil somewhere in between the two; if you are really lucky, you have loam, which is fertile, well drained and easy to work.

Clay soil

In clay soil, the individual particles in the soil are very small (less than 0.002mm) and clump together easily, forming a sticky mass. The addition of organic matter helps to prise the particles apart, allowing air to permeate and excess water to drain, so preventing the particles from sticking together again. Some gardeners advocate the addition of grit or gravel too; although research by the Royal Horticultural Society suggests that you need to incorporate a whopping 250kg of grit or gravel per square metre to have any significant effect!

The best time to dig over clay soil and incorporate organic matter is the autumn and early winter, before the onset of the wettest weather. If you have clay soil, be glad of winter frosts: alternate freezing and thawing of the soil helps to break down the heavy clods.

And in case you are thinking of giving up on your clay soil even before you start, take heart: clay soil is rich in nutrients, so it is well worth spending time unlocking them.

Sandy soil

At the other extreme from clay is sand. Sandy soil is characterized by soil particles from 0.05 to 2mm in size. This means that the soil doesn't hold much moisture, allowing water to drain away much quicker than in clay soils, and it is easy to cultivate. That's more like it, I hear you say – but hold hard: sandy soils dry out quickly and are also low in nutrients, so it's not all joy. Again, the incorporation of organic matter will improve the soil, by aiding moisture retention and helping to bind the soil particles together.

Silt soil

In between clay and sand comes silt. Silt soil has particles that range in size between 0.002 and 0.05mm, which means that the soil is fairly well drained but will hold a reasonable amount of moisture. This type of soil is far better than either clay or sand, but its main drawback is that it is easily compacted.

Loam

If you are lucky enough to have loam, the plant world is your oyster! Loam is a combination of clay, sand and silt; it is fertile, drains well but still retains moisture, and is easy to work. It is the ideal soil – the sort that dreams are made of! There are some plants that like slight variations from these conditions – for example, *Lavandula* (lavender) like very free-draining soil, whereas *Astrantia* (masterwort) can cope with quite poorly drained soil – but the majority of plants, be they bee-friendly or otherwise, thrive in a well-drained but moisture-retentive, fertile, loamy soil.

So if you haven't got that sort of soil, can you achieve it? Sadly, often the answer is that you can't – remember the saying, you can't make a silk purse out of a sow's ear? To some extent the same is true for soils. But don't despair; you can *improve* the soil you have, even if you can't totally transform it, and by improving it you will extend the range of plants you are able to grow.

Improving the soil

The most straightforward way of improving the soil is to dig in loads of organic matter in the shape of garden compost or well-rotted farmyard or stable manure. Organic matter is the heart of the soil – if it is lacking, or there is too little of it, the soil is effectively, if not literally, dead. So get as much compost or manure into the soil as you can – and keep on adding it in the shape of mulch in spring and/or autumn.

When we moved to our new house in late summer some 12 years ago the modest garden looked pristine. The builders had left it in what appeared to be an immaculate condition, with lovely, friable top soil. I started rubbing my hands with glee, imagining all the lovely flowers and vegetables that I would soon be planting out, if not immediately, then next spring. But you can't judge a book by its cover, so I started digging in two or three places and – you have probably guessed what I found. Underneath a scant three inches of top soil I struck clay in one place, rubble in another and a bag of unused (and now solid) cement in another.

After a lot of hard work we cleared and dug the garden (thank goodness it is fairly small) and I ordered two truckloads of manure from a local stable. Our neighbours thought I was totally crazy when I stood, shovel in hand and wheelbarrow at my side, posing alongside my mountain of muck while my husband took a photo for the 'house archive'. They thought I was even more crazy when, having spread the manure on the garden, I then covered it with black plastic, weighted down at the sides, and left it over the winter and well into spring. The days started to lengthen, the blackbirds started nesting, and the sun shone with just a little more vigour. Now was the time to reveal the alchemy that had been taking place underneath the plastic. Already my garden was starting to resemble a garden; the worms, having been protected from the cold and the rain over the winter, had begun to take the manure down into the soil beneath. It's true that two truckloads of manure don't make a garden, but the promise was there.

Even now, I still keep adding muck every spring and autumn – but now I don't need two truckloads each time!

Soil pH

It is vital to know if your soil is neutral, acidic or alkaline. If you have a burgeoning garden then you will already have an idea of its acidity or alkalinity, just by looking at what is thriving in it. If you are planting from scratch, have a look initially at what is doing well in your neighbours' gardens and take your cue from them. If you are in a spot where camellia, rhododendron and witch hazel flourish then your soil will be acidic; if you are surrounded by plants that have evolved from native species, like cornflowers and poppies, or are Mediterranean in origin, like lavender, then the chances are that the soil is on the alkaline side.

To find out what the pH ('potential of Hydrogen') of your soil is, it is worth investing in an inexpensive testing kit from your local garden centre, which will give you a reasonably accurate indication. A pH measurement of 6.5 to 7.0 is neutral; a measurement below this is considered acid, and one above indicates that the soil is alkaline.

Acid soil

If the pH measurement is between 3.0 and 5.0 you have very acid soil and little will grow happily in it. The best course of action is to add some lime to raise the pH to above 5.0.

If you have a reading of 5.1 to 6.0 you have acid soil, which is ideal for camellias, blueberries and the like.

Neutral soil

A pH measurement of 6.5 to 7.0 indicates that the soil is neutral, which is really good news for the majority of plants as this is the range in which nutrients are most easily available.

Alkaline soil

Alkaline soil will give you a reading of 7.1 to 8.0, which will support a number of plants – far more than if you have acid soil.

Unless your soil is at the extremity of the pH range, it is better to find plants that will cope with the nature of the soil rather than try to alter the soil to accommodate your favourite plant – the old adage of 'right plant for the right place' was never truer than when it comes to soil pH.

Shelter

More plants will thrive in a sheltered spot than in one exposed to driving wind. And more bees will visit plants growing in a sheltered area than in an exposed one. Bees are reluctant to leave the hive on a very windy day and if the only forage they can find is open to the elements it makes their lives even more difficult. If your garden is naturally sheltered you might want to skip over this section; if it's not, you may find a couple of useful tips.

In order to provide shelter in a garden you have to put a barrier between what you want to protect and the thing you want to protect it from. In reality this will mean planting a hedge or erecting a wall, fence or other construction. Which of these you ultimately decide on will be influenced by a number of factors, such as aesthetics, cost, and what benefit you hope to derive from it. Let's look at each option in turn.

Hedge

From a bee's perspective, a hedge made up of shrubs with bee-friendly flowers is by far the best option. Even better is a hedge that includes a range of shrubs that flower from spring through to autumn. A flowering – and subsequently fruiting – hedge is beneficial to a whole range of other wildlife too. Not only that, it makes a decent backdrop for anything you plant in front of it. So if you can, I would advocate planting a hedge over and above any other form of barrier or enclosure.

There are certain constraints, however. First, space: a mature hedge can take a fair slice out of your garden, so if you have a small garden to begin with, this may not be the best option. Second, cost: depending on the type of plants you choose, how mature they are when you buy them, and whether they are bare-root or container-grown, it can be quite an expensive project. Third, maintenance: a hedge is really just a group of shrubs and they will need to be fed, watered and pruned as necessary. Lastly, time: even if you buy good-sized shrubs to begin with, it will still take a number of years for your hedge to reach maturity.

Although most hedging shrubs are tough customers it is worth giving them a bit of a helping hand to get established by erecting a temporary permeable screen on the windward side. Ram some posts into the ground, about 1.8m apart, and attach some plastic windbreak to it. (This is readily available via the internet if you can't find any locally.) It might look a little unsightly to begin with but it will help no end in getting your permanent, living windbreak growing.

Wall

If you plump for a wall, your choice will depend on a number of factors. First, a wall is not as bee-friendly as a hedge – at least at first glance. It may not provide anything in the way of food for bees, but it could provide a useful habitat for solitary bees, especially if small nooks and crannies are left in it, or if it is built from a range of materials. Remember that a wall doesn't necessarily have to be made entirely from cemented brick or stone: it could be filled gabions, or, as demonstrated in a show garden at Chelsea recently, it could be a dry stone wall with sections made up of various insect habitats, including old books!

Second, your selection will hinge to some degree on where you live and what sort of material is available in your area. If you live in a flint cottage then rendered concrete might not be the best choice, whereas if you live in a modern townhouse it may be just the ticket. Third, there is the cost: any sort of wall will be relatively expensive not only because of the materials but also because of the labour involved in building it. Lastly, unless your wall has gaps in it, wind will hit a stone or brick wall and be channelled over the top, forming an eddy the other side which can cause as much damage to plants as leaving them directly exposed to the wind.

Fence

A fence is probably the first choice of windbreak for the majority of people but as far as being bee-friendly goes, it would get *nul points* in a Eurovision

Barrier Contest! There are other considerations, though. First, a wooden fence will 'fit in' to almost any garden, traditional or modern. Second, the materials are relatively cheap to buy and even a moderately good DIY-er can tackle putting one up. (Please make sure, however, that the timber has been approved by the Forest Stewardship Council (FSC) or other similar body.) Third, it has to be maintained, and even with regular maintenance its life-span is not great. Fourth, if you decide on a fence, make sure it has a broken surface. By that I don't mean that it's about to fall down, but that it has gaps in it so that the wind can filter through it. The strength of the wind can be reduced by up to 50 per cent by putting a filtering mechanism in its way.

Water

The obvious source of water in any garden is rainfall. Wouldn't it be wonderful if we lived in some sort of utopia, where it only rained at night, and we all got just enough rainfall on a regular basis, year round, to sustain our plants? The reality is quite different, of course. We always seem to have too much or not enough.

The best way to deal with this situation is to choose plants that can cope with our own regional and local conditions. All the same, it is wise to try to conserve as much as possible of a precious resource like water when we have an abundance to sustain plants that need a little extra. These plants include those in containers, or newly planted ones in the border that need a bit of help until they are established and can fend for themselves. For the average gardener the best way to hoard extra water is to install one or more butts to collect rainwater from the roof of the house, garage or outbuildings. I have three 'in tandem' collecting water from the house. When the first one is full, it overflows into the second one and so on. Generally this is enough for all my watering needs, except on the rarest occasion when I have resorted to mains water.

2
Designing with Plants

General design aspects of planting schemes

We have looked at the conditions in your garden and at this stage it may be tempting to choose all your favourite plants and end up with a border full of shrubs, say, with a few perennials thrown in – and if that's what pleases you (and the bees!) then go for it! However, if you are interested in a more balanced design it is worth adopting a more ordered approach. This is where looking at some principles of design might help.

Like any other field of design, there are some guidelines that are worth taking into account when designing a bee-friendly border. I say guidelines, because they are just that, rather than prescriptive rules, and you can use them, adjust them – or ignore them! – just as you please in order to achieve a design that satisfies you, the conditions of your space, and the bees that you are hoping to attract.

There are certain principles of design that help us to create a satisfying plan. When you view a border and it 'looks right' the chances are that all of these principles are working together to create a harmonious unity. It is not that you would consciously go through a list and tick them all off, but your subconscious would be telling you that this border is pleasing to the eye. These principles include things like balance, focalization, movement, proportion and repetition.

What about colour, or texture, then? Where do they fit in? Colour and texture, along with form, line and scale, are the elements, or tools of design, that we can use in various combinations to adjust the principles of design. In effect, you can use elements to 'produce' principles, but you cannot use principles to bring about elements. For example, you can use colour and line to achieve balance, but you cannot use balance to achieve colour or line.

The design suggestions I have made are not set in stone; many designers use different approaches, but I have found that if I keep some design principles in mind, it helps me to focus my thoughts. Let's have a look at my suggested principles and elements of design to see how they can affect the way we design or view a border attractive to bees.

Principles of design

Proportion

Generally speaking, we don't register that things are in proportion to one another – we only take notice when they are out of proportion. In the garden, one example is when a plant is put in a pot that is far too big for it, or vice versa: it doesn't look right. What we want to achieve is a harmonious relation of one thing to another. We see things as being in proportion when they sit comfortably with each other.

Balance

We recognize that a design is balanced if one side is equal to the other. If the balance is symmetrical, one side is exactly the same as the other side. This sort of balance can occur in a border when one half of the planting scheme is replicated in the other half along a central axis. You have to be careful with this type of planting, however, because it can look contrived and a little boring unless it is in a very formal setting.

A design can be balanced without being exactly the same on both sides, however. Asymmetrical balance uses different sizes, forms, colours and textures to obtain *visual* balance, not necessarily *actual* balance. Most borders will be asymmetrically balanced. For example, a large shrub at one end of a border may be balanced by a grouping of several smaller, evergreen perennials at the other.

Focalization

Focal points are used as punctuation marks, capturing our attention and helping our eye to negotiate the array of planting that is set before us. For example, in a border a focal point might be a specimen tree or shrub.

Movement

The way in which we perceive gradual or abrupt change can generate a sense of movement, both fast and slow, along a border. Careful use of colour, line and form can bring about a feeling of motion, which leads your eye through or even beyond the area.

Repetition

Repetition hardly needs explanation! In a border you can repeat a combination of plants to help bring about an overall unity; for example, groups of three or five ornamental alliums, placed at intervals along a border, can create a sense of coherence. Be careful, though, because too much repetition can be monotonous.

Elements of design

When we are thinking about planting a new border or updating an existing one, the thing that often springs to mind first is colour. This is an important consideration, but it is not the only one. We have to think about other elements too, such as form, scale and texture. As much as we may like tall plants with feathery foliage and yellow flowers, a whole border of them would look dramatic to begin with but would soon look uninspiring and, frankly, boring. You could argue, of course, that if they happen to be bee-friendly ones, that would be justification enough, since bees do like masses of similar flowers, but our aim is to not only attract bees into the garden but to make it attractive to humans too. So let's have a look at some of the elements we need to consider.

Colour

Colour is probably the thing that strikes us most when we look at a border. Colours can bring about different feelings and emotions: 'hot' colours such as red or orange can excite or enliven us; 'cool' colours such as blue can create a feeling of calm. Colours can also appear to advance or recede. For example, 'hot' colours appear to advance towards the eye, whereas 'cool' colours sometimes all but disappear. And no colour stands alone – it is always seen in relation to other colours; have a look at Figure 1, a simplified colour wheel.

It is an accepted design precept that colours that are opposite one another on the colour wheel will look good together (complementary colours), as will colours that adjoin one another (analogous colours). But it is also worth experimenting with different colour combinations and juxtapositions – sometimes the most surprising groupings look fantastic. The late Christopher Lloyd wowed visitors to his garden at Great Dixter with dramatic colour schemes that any lesser a plantsman would have steered clear of.

Figure 1 A simplified colour wheel

Form

We often use the terms 'shape' and 'form' together, and they have come to be regarded as interchangeable. (If we want to be pedantic, we would say that form is to do with the three-dimensional characteristics of a volume, whereas shape is to do with the outline or two-dimensional characteristics of something.) The form of a plant, including its flowers and foliage, can have a direct effect on how we perceive a border. For example, using a plant with fine leaves in a small area will increase the feeling of space; using large-leaved plants at the end of a long, narrow border will make the space feel shorter.

Line

A line can serve to join, link, support, surround, or intersect other things. Conceptually, it has length but no width or depth. A line can express direction and movement; it can be straight or curved, cutting across a composition to create a division, or uniting areas and creating a more relaxed atmosphere. In a border you can run a thread of one type of plant through a border to link the whole area together, a device that is often used in naturalistic planting.

Scale

If we are thinking about proportion, we are looking at things in relation to one another, regardless of their size; the same is partly true of scale, except that instead of looking at things in relation to one another, we are comparing them to a particular item of a specific size. In the garden – and just about every other situation we come across – our particular item of a specific size is the average human being: this is our 'reference standard'. In our everyday lives we judge things and orientate ourselves according to our own size. We do come across other scales, of course; think of a miniature railway or a doll's house. With these, we recognize immediately that there is a different 'reference standard' at play and we alter our perception of the whole thing accordingly.

Scale and proportion are closely linked because it is only once we know what scale is being used, or to what 'reference standard' we are comparing something, that we can judge whether one thing is in proportion to another. Taking the doll's house as an example, if we put a 'human' scale teaspoon on a doll's house scale table, then we know straight away that the teaspoon is totally out of proportion to the rest of the setting; we have recognized that a different 'reference standard' is in place.

Texture

The texture of an object is its surface quality that can be felt (actual) or seen (visual). Texture cannot always be easily described; an infinite number of adjectives could be used – matt, shiny, rough, smooth, ribbed, lacy, feathery, pitted, velvety, furry, coarse, prickly, spiky, scaly, silky, hairy, sticky, waxy, thorny, flaky, rubbery, papery, wiry, crinkly, fissured, downy … the list is almost endless!

In the garden, we may think that we recognize a plant's texture by touch, but in fact we first register its texture visually. All may not be as it appears, however. Actual and visual texture may differ considerably. A striped leaf may appear to be ribbed, yet to the touch it is perfectly smooth. This is something to bear in mind when deciding which plants to use in a design.

Time

Time stands apart from any principle or element of design. In the short term, we have to consider the seasonality of plants – at what time of year will they look their most outstanding and be of most use to bees? In the long term, we need a rough idea of the time it will take for the plants to fill the space, and also how long it will be before the border begins to look tired and past its best.

Does it look right?

If all this sounds too involved and technical, don't worry. When we look at a border, we give very little conscious thought to nearly everything that I have described in detail above. We either like or dislike the way the planting looks and feels, and that is enough. But as an experiment, the next time you visit a garden and look at a border, especially one that you *don't* like, have a think about what it is that doesn't quite look right. I would wager that one or more of the principles of design are out of kilter.

A useful method of composing a design

It's now time to look at how we can choose different types of plants to create an attractive, bee-friendly border. A tried and tested method is to select plants according to their function, which generally means that you can split them into four categories: Focus, Framework, Flowers, and Fillers. These 'Four Fs' become the embodiment of the design principles and elements that we have just been looking at.

Focus

The focus is the plant (usually a tree or large shrub) that acts as a focal point in the planting space. You should take care to select a plant that is visually strong but does not overwhelm the space: in other words, it needs to be in proportion to the rest of the planting or the garden as a whole.

A focus should command attention all year round; even when the bees are having 'time off' during the winter months, we still need something good to look at in the depth of winter. If your planting area isn't large enough to cope with an imposing focus, opt for a smaller specimen.

Framework plants

Framework plants are usually shrubs, both evergreen and deciduous, which are used to create a framework within the border. Like the focus plant, framework plants have to be in proportion to their plant neighbours. Imagine a bed of alpine plants with a two-metre conifer growing out of the middle of it – not a pretty sight! Framework plants can also help to balance the scheme: I mentioned above how one large shrub could be balanced visually by a group of smaller plants. They can also lead the eye along the border, creating movement from one focal point to another.

Framework plants provide year-round structure, with interesting flowers, foliage, stems or berries at various times.

Flowers

This group consists mainly of herbaceous perennials, which come into their own from the late spring, through summer to the autumn months, with their flowers providing a riot of colour, texture and form.

Flowers are perhaps the most hard-working element when it comes to design: their design attributes (like colour, texture and form) can be used in many different ways – subtly or boldly, traditionally or ingeniously, densely or sparingly – to create a design in which all the principles come into play.

Strictly speaking, herbaceous perennials are plants that do not have woody stems; this category encompasses those plants that die down each autumn to reappear the following spring, but also tends to include perennials with evergreen foliage, some herbs, and, occasionally, alpines and bulbs. In addition, some plants which are strictly shrubs or sub-shrubs, like *Lavandula* or *Perovskia*, are often included in this category.

The way in which flowers are used can affect the 'feel' of the design, from dramatic to hotchpotch. Blocks or drifts of the same plant can look stunning (and are brilliant for bees) but this can take a little courage to put into practice. At the other end of the planting spectrum is the collection of single plants which carry a meaningful association for the gardener, or have been bought simply because they looked good – this is fine for the gardener but not so good for the bees. I would encourage anyone who is planting a new border, or refreshing an old one, to plant perennials in groups of a minimum of three. From a design, and the bee's, point of view, this is a good practice to adopt.

Fillers

Filler planting gives instant colour and drama exactly where it is needed. Bulbs, annuals, self-seeding plants, biennials and some tender perennials fall into this category. They can be sown or planted where there is a gap or be grown in pots and placed where there is a space. By filling in the gaps, these plants can provide an immediate, albeit transitory, focal point, or create movement through a border, and they are past masters at repetition.

Spring fillers

In the spring, bulbs can be relied upon to bring come colour to the border, and some desperately needed food for the bees. *Crocus* are especially good, while tulips, although they may not be top of the bee's food favourites, provide a good amount of pollen, and from a design point of view, give us a reliable season of colour and form.

And don't forget *Erysimum cheiri* (wallflowers). This useful perennial, invariably grown as a biennial, was once a stalwart of spring bedding, giving a beautiful, scented display – and lots of nectar and pollen – during April and May. It seems to have been superseded by pansies and polyanthus nowadays, since they can be relied upon to give colour much earlier and for longer than the wallflower. But our gain is the bees' loss because they yield next to nothing in terms of bee food. Wallflowers are an excellent filler plant, too, so bear them in mind when you are deciding on your planting scheme.

Summer and autumn fillers

Summer and autumn are the seasons when the annuals, in particular, come into their own. There are many to choose from but my personal favourites are *Nigella*, the annual *Echium* – *E.* 'Blue Bedder' – and *Phacelia*. In Germany, the latter is known as *Bienenfreund* – bee-friend – an apt name if ever there was one!

Ornamental onions, Allium, also provide quantities of nectar during the early summer, and they make superb fillers.

How the 'Four Fs' fit together

In order to give you some idea of how the 'Four Fs' fit together in a plan without worrying about specific plants, I have provided an illustration of a border in a simple diagrammatic form (see Figure 2). Here we have a focus, balanced by three framework 'plants', with flowers making up the bulk of the space, and some fillers in between. By paring the forms down to basic shapes we can already see how each of the categories fits into the overall scheme.

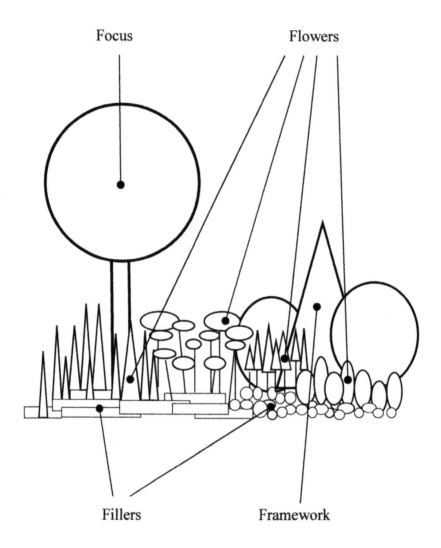

Figure 2 How the 'Four Fs' fit together

Adapting this method to your space

A point to remember is that you may not necessarily have examples of all four categories of plants in your planting plan, especially if you are designing/redesigning a fairly simple border. A focus plant is just that – something special to focus on, and you may not have more than one focus plant in your entire garden, let alone in each border. Your space may favour a large grouping of framework plants, or you may wish to have a space containing just flowers; you may feel that filler plants are unnecessary.

When planning your planting you need to take into account the mature height and spread of each plant. This will necessarily affect the number of plants that you can comfortably fit into a planting space. Trees and shrubs will obviously take a long time to achieve maturity (some of them many years), whereas many of the perennials will start to become overcrowded or deteriorate after three or four years, at which time you can dig them up and divide them. Some perennials may need to be replaced after only a couple of years. By contrast, the bulk of 'filler' plants will be at their best in the same year that you plant them.

Remember these points when you plant up your new border, and don't worry if you have bare ground in places – the flowers will grow into the spaces, and meanwhile, that is what your fillers are for.

This is only one method of designing a border, and as long as you keep the needs of the bees to the forefront of your mind it is your choice what you include; even if you feel, subsequently, that you have made a mistake, you can move or remove plants accordingly.

3
Bee Specifics

General ways to make your garden more bee-friendly

Although we are concentrating on plants for bees in this book, it is worth looking very briefly at some general factors that can make the garden as a whole more bee-friendly – things like providing water, and suitable habitats for bumblebees and solitary bees; and, if you wish to keep honeybees for yourself, appropriate locations for beehives.

Water for bees

Like every other living creature, bees cannot do without water; if we can provide a reliable source for them in our garden it removes the need for them to search elsewhere. You don't need a pond – although if you do have the space for one it will attract no end of wildlife – as bees cannot land on water without breaking the meniscus (the 'taut' surface of the water) and they are not good swimmers! Bees will take water from any wet surface, such as grass, pebbles and even wet washing, rather than from open water.

Ideally bees like a solid surface to land and walk on to get to the water. In practice this can be achieved by placing pebbles or crocks in a watertight container and filling it up with clean water to just below the surface of the pebbles. Be sure to keep the container topped up, though; it's surprising how much water a honeybee colony needs – up to four litres a day in some instances! I make a habit of replenishing the 'bee water' whenever I water my containers of plants, which, even during a rainy spell, I do at least once a day.

Bees are creatures of habit when it comes to water. Once they have found a suitable and reliable source, they are very reluctant to go elsewhere. You are likely to see other insects, birds and mammals coming to the 'watering hole' – I have even seen my neighbour's elderly cat quenching her thirst at mine, although she was rather put out by being 'dive-bombed' by a bumblebee trying to get to the water!

Habitats for bumblebees and other bees

Even if you don't keep honeybees yourself, or there isn't a colony nearby, you are bound to find bees of some description in your garden. The obvious ones are the 'fluffy' bumblebees, but you will no doubt find solitary bees and other insects such as hoverflies. All of these have a role to play in the ecological balance of your garden, so they should be encouraged to visit and even make their home there. For advice on providing homes for bumblebees, contact the Bumblebee Conservation Trust (address at the end of the book).

Although you can buy 'nest boxes' for bumblebees and other bees, research has shown that these are frequently overlooked in favour of a site that the bees have found for themselves – so don't be disappointed if your bijou bee residence remains empty! Some solitary bees nest in hollow stems, like bamboo canes or larger herbaceous plant stems. Others nest in the ground in bare soil or short turf, so if you see little mounds of soil appearing, don't immediately think you have mice – it could be the beginnings of a solitary bee nest.

Siting a honeybee hive

You may like to keep honeybees yourself. It is beyond the scope of this book to look at how exactly to do this (see Further Reading for books on beekeeping), but here are a few guidelines that will help you to find the best place to put your hive, or hives, in your garden – which, hopefully, already has a good source of food in the form of bee-friendly flowers.

- Try to find somewhere tucked away – don't place your hive in a position where you, your family or friends will be walking close to it on a regular basis.
- Place your hive in the sun (but dappled shade will do at a push), preferably facing south.
- Find a position that is sheltered from the wind.
- Avoid frost hollows.
- Make sure the site is not prone to flooding.
- Don't place your hive under a tree – drooping branches knocking against the hive, and water droplets falling on it during and after rain, will annoy the bees.
- Make sure that you keep the area around the hive free of weeds and

grass, which may hinder the bees when they leave and return to the hive. Cut back the grass and weeds – on no account use a weedkiller!

• If you live in an urban area, or where you think your neighbours might be worried by the bees, place your hive in an enclosed space, partially surrounded by a fence or wall. This will encourage the bees to fly well above head height until they reach the vicinity of the hive.

This list might seem a little long, but most of it is common sense when you look at it from a bee's point of view.

What makes a plant bee-friendly?

When it comes to designing a planting scheme for bees, some aspects of the design considerations that we looked at earlier are more important than others. Three stand out, over and above the others, and they are the form of the flower, the colour of the flower, and what time of year the plant blooms. We need, therefore, to give these particular thought when we start putting ideas together for different borders.

I have gone into detail elsewhere about what sort of plants are best for bees and what flowers produce in the way of foodstuff for bees (see *The Bee Garden* – details in Further Reading), but it is worth including here some characteristics of the most suitable plants, especially for honeybees, so that we can be prepared when we come to choose plants for our borders.

I have devised the following short mnemonic to use as a sort of checklist to keep in mind when deciding what sort of plants are best for our buzzy friends:

Friends Are Very Special

You may be wondering what this has to do with plants – although I have to say some of my plants do feel like very special friends – but I will briefly explain, and then look at in a little more detail, each of the components:

F = food
A = accessibility
V = visibility
S = seasonality

Food

Why do bees visit flowers in the first place? Flowers provide food for bees in the shape of pollen and nectar; these two items, along with water, are the only foodstuffs bees need to survive. In a nutshell, it is the pollen, which is produced by the male sex organs of the plant, that supplies bees with the protein that they need for the proper growth and repair of their bodies. Nectar, on the other hand, provides bees with carbohydrate in the form of a sugary liquid which is secreted by plant nectaries.

Nectaries can be either 'floral', which means that they are found within the flower, or 'extra-floral' – located outside the flower, usually but not always at the point where a leaf joins the stem. For pollen-bearing plants, floral nectaries are of the greatest importance because the nectar attracts pollinating insects to the flower. Floral nectaries are usually found in the heart of the flower, which means that the insect has to brush past the pollen-bearing stamens to get to the nectar. In effect, the nectar is the insect's reward for being 'hijacked' by the flower to distribute its pollen.

Therefore, the more plants we choose that offer a good supply of pollen and/or nectar, the greater the number of bees that will be attracted to our garden.

Accessibility

There are thousands of different flowers providing varying amounts of pollen and/or nectar; a cursory glance around a well-stocked garden in the summer, buzzing with insects, is testament to that. Certain types of flowers, however, seem to attract bees more than others. This is because not only do the bees know that there is food waiting for them; more importantly, they know that they can *access* it.

Whether or not bees can access pollen or nectar depends on the form of the flower.

Single flowers are best

There is one particular, and very important, aspect of flower form that we need to be aware of when we are deciding which plants are best for bees: it is invariably *single* flowers that our buzzy friends make a bee-line for. It is rare for double flowers to provide much, if anything, in the way of bee food; the extra petals of a double flower are really a genetic mutation of the sexual structures of the flower, which means that there are no, or very few, pollen-bearing male stamens and often no nectaries. If a bee did visit, its journey would be all but wasted.

The shape of the flower

If the flower is open or cup-shaped it is very straightforward for bees to get to both pollen and nectar. If the flower is tube-shaped, however, where the petals have fused to form a corolla tube, the nectar may not be so easy to reach. Indeed, the corolla tubes of some flowers are so deep that some bees cannot access the nectar at all; only bumblebees (and sometimes only butterflies) are able to reach it. This is because of the difference in the length of the proboscis (the long, slender 'tongue' of nectar-supping insects, which acts as a straw).

As a general rule, if a flower is suitable for honeybees then it is highly likely to be acceptable to the vast number of other nectar-sipping and pollinating insects. I saw an example of this when I visited a garden in the north of England in late September. A swathe of *Agastache* 'Black Adder' had been planted which was proving irresistible not only to honeybees but

Figure 3	Figure 4
Agastache and Red Admiral butterflies	*Agastache* and the white-tailed bumblebee

to Red Admiral butterflies (*Vanessa atalanta*) and the white-tailed bumblebee (*Bombus lucorum*) – all delighted in the abundant nectar (see Figures 3 and 4).

We look in more detail below at what families of plants are best for bees, but as a general guideline, plants with daisy or 'pincushion' flowers – like *Echinacea* sp and *Knautia* sp, respectively – where there are numerous small flowers collected together on one head, are really good for bees. Those with lots of individual flowers held on spikes (like *Lavandula* sp) are also attractive, as are larger, open flowers, like single species of *Rosa* (rose) and *Fragaria* sp (strawberry).

Native flowers

What has become clear to me, as a beekeeper as well as a gardener, is that the nearer a plant is in form to its 'wild', original species, the more attractive it is to bees. This is because the original species have evolved naturally, without human interference, to attract the pollinating insect that is best suited to their needs. Some plants have evolved to such a degree that they can only be pollinated by one particular agent. For example, the Chinese orchid, *Cymbidium serratum*, is only pollinated by a wild mountain mouse, *Rattus fulvescens* – yes, a mouse! I don't think any of our native species have evolved quite that far, but it is true to say that the flower of each native species has developed to draw the attention of a suitable pollinator.

This doesn't mean, of course, that we should only plant native species in our gardens. Many cultivated varieties are not only attractive to us but they are also good for bees. So, hopefully, we can have the best of both worlds.

Visibility

We looked at colour from a design perspective in Chapter 2, but we need to consider the extra dimension of bees' vision in order to see how this might affect how we go about choosing plants for our bee-friendly borders.

Bees 'see' differently from humans. We can see all the colours of the rainbow, from red through to violet (750–370 nanometres (nm)); bees see less than us at one end of the colour spectrum but more than us at the other end (650–300 nm). Bees do not see red (620–750nm) as we do, and we cannot see ultraviolet (300–370nm).

Bees' vision is complex, and although they can detect a fairly broad range of colours, what they see is less differentiated than what we see. This has a direct influence on which flowers bees are attracted to: they will automatically target flowers that stand out to them.

The illustration in Figure 5 is a slightly different sort of colour wheel: in the centre are the colours that we can see, and this is compared with how bees might see these colours, around the outside.

This is not to say that we should dismiss any colour out of hand, though: just because a flower might appear to us to be outside the bees'

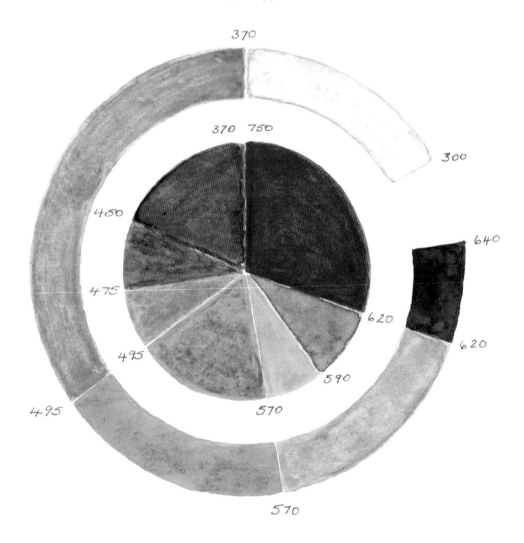

Figure 5 Visual spectrum colour wheel

visual spectrum, it doesn't mean that it might not be appealing to them. Although we may think, from the colour of the petals, that the flowers are 'invisible' to bees, it is often the case that the centre of the flower, where the 'business area' is located, is of a colour that is well within the bees' field of vision, especially if we take into account the part of the spectrum that we humans can't see – ultraviolet.

Flowers often have marks on their petals of a contrasting colour to the rest of the flower, or they contain UV 'pigments', which guide the bee to where the nectar can be found, in much the same way as airstrips have landing lights for planes. These markings are known as nectar guides.

The idea that the best form of a flower for bees is one that is closest to its native species also seems to apply to colour. Many cultivated varieties of flowers have been bred to be attractive to the human eye, but the colours of wild flowers seem to be consistent with the colours that their respective pollinators can best see.

Bees are able to detect movements at a much faster rate than humans. Bees' eyes are compound eyes, made up of thousands of tiny lenses; these collect images that are then combined by the brain into one large picture. They can also easily distinguish between solid and broken patterns, with a preference for the latter. A mass of perennials waving slightly in a gentle breeze will be an easy target for the honeybee, and when they do start to forage, they don't have to move very far from one pollen and nectar source to another. It is therefore best to position perennials and annuals in groups or blocks rather than as single specimens. There is not the same necessity to do this with trees and shrubs, however, because they carry many flowers on one plant.

Seasonality

Honeybees start to appear in March or April, depending on the temperature and general weather conditions. If you see a bee buzzing about the garden in late winter or very early spring and the temperature is below 6°C, then it will probably be a bumblebee of some description because honeybees will not venture outside the hive unless the temperature is above this level. Honeybees will continue flying until the first frosts, which can occur any time between late September and early December. Usually, however, once the abundant nectar that is produced by ivy flowers late in the season has been gathered, there will be very few bees around until next spring.

It is important to aim to provide food for bees and other insects for as long a period as possible when they are active. Much of the time this depends on the weather, of course. A hot, dry spring will bring an abundance of pollen and nectar, which enables honeybees to build up their colonies, but if this is followed by a cold, wet summer, with a resulting dearth of food, the colony will suffer and they may not be able to accumulate enough stores to last them through the winter. Vigilant beekeepers will be aware of this, and will provide them with specially formulated bee food to make sure that they have enough. Gardeners can't do an awful lot to mitigate the weather-induced lack of flowers, however – we can't control the climate!

The 'June gap'

Even in a 'normal' year, when we end up with the sort of weather we might expect, there are periods throughout the growing season when the border can look a little sparse. I am thinking particularly of what beekeepers call the 'June gap', when the abundance of spring flowers is exhausted but the early summer flush of blooms is yet to appear. (This 'in-between' period may not necessarily occur in June, of course; it is entirely dependent on the weather.) The 'changeover' between summer and autumn, too, can see the border looking a little thin.

We gardeners, however, can have a trick up our sleeve which might go a modest way towards alleviating the problem. Unlike a magician's ruse, where one minute you don't see it and the next minute you do, we have to think ahead a little – in fact, several weeks ahead – and sow a succession of annual seeds. By doing this we can provide a limited, but possibly crucial, supply of short-term bee-friendly plants to fill in the gaps in the border. Of course, if the weather is truly against us, even this ploy won't work, but for the sake of a few pounds (or, even better, having saved some seed from last year's pollinated flowers), it may provide just the snack the bees need until the next proper course appears.

Bees' favourite plant families

By now I hope you are feeling a little more confident about choosing plants for your bee border, and about putting them together in a pleasing way. Nevertheless, there is one more suggestion that might be worth bearing in mind when it comes to choosing specific plants.

Having looked at a whole range of bee-friendly plants, it seems that a good number of them fall into two main families – enough to call them 'Primary' families (Asteraceae and Lamiaceae). There are four other families that have a good variety of bee-friendly plants in their ranks, and I have categorized these as 'Secondary' families (Boraginaceae, Ranunculaceae, Rosaceae and Scrophulariaceae). Many other plant families also contain bee-friendly plants, but there are fewer instances in each of them, so in addition to the Primary and Secondary families, there is another group, in which I have lumped together lots of other families, which I have called 'Other'.

From a design perspective, if you make sure that some of your focus plants, framework plants, flowers and fillers in your planting plan come from both of the Primary families, along with a few from the Secondary families, you will already have an interesting combination of texture and form, and you will be sure to have a bee-friendly mixture. If you have a larger area to fill, you can intersperse the Primaries with many more from the Secondary families and also include some 'Other' plants if you wish.

In each of the groupings below the families are arranged in alphabetical order. You will find a list of plant species arranged according to their family, for easy reference, in Appendix 1.

Primary families

If I had to choose the top bee-friendly plant families for ornamental – rather than commercial or edible – value, they would be Asteraceae and Lamiaceae. These two families contain a huge range of plants that are of utmost value to bees.

Asteraceae

The Asteraceae family used to be called Compositae, which gives a clue to the type of flowers it produces. The flower heads are a composite of lots of individual flowers; these can either be regular, with all the petals the same size, often forming corolla tubes (like the cornflower, *Centaurea cyanus*), or they can be irregular, with some petals bigger than others (like sunflowers, *Helianthus annuus*). Many members of the Asteraceae family produce prodigious amounts of pollen, and there is also a very useful 'landing platform' for the bees to touch down on!

Lamiaceae

Typical flowers of the Lamiaceae family have petals that have fused together into an upper and lower lip (which gave rise to the family's former name of Labiatae), and are positioned in clusters around the stem. This means that the bee can visit scores of individual flowers on one stem to collect nectar, using very little energy and pollinating numerous flowers at the same time. The plants are often aromatic; many herbs, such as lavender (*Lavandula* sp), rosemary (*Rosmarinus* sp), mint (*Mentha* sp), marjoram (*Origanum vulgare*) and sage (*Salvia* sp) belong to this family.

Secondary families

Although not containing as many bee-friendly plants as the Primary families, Secondary families include a vast number of plants that are popular with both gardeners and bees.

Boraginaceae

This family contains over 2,000 species, some of which are very useful bee plants – one of which, not surprisingly, is *Borago officinalis* (borage). Others include *Anchusa officinalis* (common bugloss or alkanet), *Symphytum* (comfrey), *Myosotis* (forget-me-not), *Heliotropium* (heliotrope), *Pulmonaria* sp and *Echium vulgare* (viper's bugloss). The majority have blue or purple flowers, and hairy stems and leaves. A number of them are herbs and some are used for dye, or medicinally.

Ranunculaceae

The Ranunculaceae family contains a wide range of wild and garden flowers such as buttercups, celandine, *Anemone, Clematis,* and *Aconitum*. The flowers may be solitary, like buttercups, or they may be held on spikes, like *Aconitum,* or in clusters. Many species in this family have no proper petals – it is the brightly coloured calyces that we mistakenly call the flower.

Rosaceae

The Rosaceae family contains not only the rose (*Rosa* sp), but also many fruit-bearing plants that are worth growing in the ornamental border: species such as apples (*Malus* sp), cherries (*Prunus* sp), pears (*Pyrus* sp), and strawberries (*Fragaria* sp) all belong to this family. Other ornamental species include *Cotoneaster*, *Geum*, rowan (*Sorbus aucuparia*) and whitebeam (*Sorbus aria*). Nearly all the flowers of the Rosaceae family are regular, with five petals that form a cup-like structure, which makes it very easy for bees to reach both pollen and nectar; the flowers are nearly always carried as clusters (think of apple blossom), which means that bees can visit lots of flowers within a short distance of one another.

Scrophulariaceae

Bee-friendly plants in the Scrophulariaceae family include *Digitalis*, *Verbascum*, *Penstemon*, *Veronica* and *Hebe*. Nearly all the members of this family have flowers that are arranged on spikes, which means that the bee can visit a number of flowers without having to fly too far. This family contains a vast number of garden-worthy plants, too.

Other families

Many individual species that don't belong to any of the Primary or Secondary families are, nonetheless, particularly useful to bees. These are listed in Appendices 1 and 2. Although the families to which each of them belongs may contain more bee-friendly plants than I have selected, the ones that I have chosen are, to my mind, most suitable to be included in an ornamental planting scheme.

4

The Plans

In this chapter I have drawn on the information we have accumulated in the previous chapters to produce a range of planting plans that I hope will enable you to create your own bee-friendly space. You can either copy the ideas as they stand or use the plans as an inspirational springboard to produce your own, unique, design.

General features of the plans

Favourite plants

As any garden designer will tell you, you quickly develop a range of 'core' plants that you are drawn to and which become your 'signature' plants; most of these, and often all of them, crop up in just about every design you create. I am no exception! You will see *Allium, Lavandula* (lavender – especially the variety 'Hidcote'), *Echinacea, Aster, Geranium, Achillea* and no end of herbs appearing repeatedly in my plans, and I make no apology for this: they are all excellent garden plants and, more importantly from my point of view, they are first-rate bee plants. You will no doubt have your favourites, too, and with luck these will be good for bees; if they aren't, you might find yourself persuaded to replace them with bee-friendly choices – after all, a border that is good for bees is what we want to achieve!

Plants that are easy to obtain

I have been careful to use plants that are fairly easy to obtain – from nurseries, garden centres or online. There are new introductions and 'choice' varieties to be had, but if they are not easy to source, or if they cost a king's ransom when you can find them, there is little point in including them, in my opinion.

Plant omissions

You may detect some omissions. I am thinking of *Hedera* (ivy) in particular. This is a bee plant *par excellence*, providing abundant nectar late in the season when the bees are topping up their stores to last them over the winter. Although I would never discourage anyone from planting a new specimen in their garden, it takes some time (15 years in some instances) to reach the mature stage when it will produce flower heads. For this reason alone I would let the bees venture into parks and countryside to source it and its nectar.

You will also discover that I have included very few trees in the planting plans. This is not because they are no good for bees – quite the contrary, in some instances; it is rather that few gardens can play host to more than one good-sized tree. So instead of suggesting specific trees I have listed a number of selected, bee-friendly ones in the table of plants at Appendix 2 – you will find them under the 'Focus' headings.

Plant spacing

The amount of space I have allowed for each grouping of plants is roughly the area they will cover two or three years after planting; don't worry if when newly planted they look a little sparse. You can supplement the planting with fillers, such as annuals and bulbs, at least for the first couple of years.

Soil and aspect

Unless the plans are specifically for particular conditions (such as acid soil or shade), I have assumed that the soil is neutral, moist but free-draining, and that the site is either full sun, or in sun for a good part of the day.

Seasonality

You will notice that the plants I have chosen, when taken together, cover the foraging period of the bees, namely spring to autumn. There is a chart for each of the plans which shows the season each plant is in flower. This is only a guide, and you may find that some plants defy their expected flowering season, starting blooming early, or going on flowering a lot later than anticipated – much depends on the weather. You could also get a second flush of blooms from early flowering plants that have been cut back after flowering: this frequently happens with *Geranium*, for example.

Many of the plants I have chosen are evergreen, so there will still be some interest during the winter period; of those that are not, a number have interesting seed heads that can be left on the plant over the winter to provide food for birds, and nesting places for insects such as ladybirds.

Size of plans

The plans vary in size from a hanging basket up to a border measuring 5.5 metres by 6 metres – with lots of variations in between – to show that however large or small your planting space is, you can provide something to sustain our buzzy friends.

Plan keys

Rather than trying to put a lot of information on each plan, you will find that areas are designated with letters and/or numbers. You will find the corresponding letter and/or number in the planting schedule that accompanies each plan, so you can see precisely what suggestions I have made, and how many of each plant you will need. I have also indicated the scale, where appropriate.

Illustrations

A number of illustrative photographs accompany each of the plans; these give you a good idea of what some of the individual varieties of plants look like. The corresponding number of the plant in the plan key appears in brackets after the name of the plant.

Not every single plant in each plan is illustrated; however, some plants are used in more than one plan, so it is worth checking the Index of Illustrated Plants (see page 194) to see whether a particular plant is shown elsewhere in the book.

There are a few sketches that give an impression as to how part of the plan might look; these are purely for illustration and are not to scale. Note that the colours used in both the plans and the sketches are for illustration only and should not be taken as literal.

Categories of plans

I have divided the plans into the following categories:

- **Garden Styles**, with plans for two traditional borders, two cottage gardens, one designer border, three 'naturalistic' borders, and a shrub border.

- **Colour Themes**, containing plans for blue and yellow, and red and yellow borders, plus a rainbow border.

- **Garden Conditions**, where you will find plans to suit acid and alkaline soils, together with a plan for a shady area.

- **Utility Gardens**, which contains practical as well as decorative use of spaces – a cutting garden, a herb garden and garden filled with flowers, fruit and vegetables.

- **A Beekeeper's Garden**, with a plan for an entire garden. This brings together, in a real garden, some of the individual plans – a culmination and realization of all the conceptual and theoretical ideas and suggestions that we have looked at.

- **Container Planting**, with ideas and suggestions for planting in containers: seasonal planting and a herb hanging basket.

Garden Styles

This section begins with two 'traditional' borders which contain the customary shrubs, perennials, annuals and bulbs – the sort of plants you would perhaps expect to find in a border. The next two plans are for 'cottage gardens', which incorporate fruit and herbs as well as flowers. There is then a 'designer' border which is a little more modern in its design approach. After that we have three 'naturalistic' borders, which are less formal and less strictly controlled than the others. Finally there is a plan for a border using shrubs and little else.

Above: Heliotropium arborescens (A – see page 38)
Left: Verbascum 'Cherry Helen' (12 – see page 38)

Large Traditional Border

This border is traditional in the sense that it contains a shrub and a climber as well as perennial and annual plants. You won't find any grasses here, not because they are not attractive or useful additions from a design point of view, but because they are far from being bee-friendly plants, as they rely on the wind for pollination rather than insects.

It is one of the largest of the plans, covering an area 6 metres by 2 metres; even so, the range and number of plants that will comfortably sit in such a space is still quite limited.

Focus

Despite the fact that a number of types of small tree could be included in the space to act as a focus, I have resisted the temptation. Once the tree is in full leaf, a large amount of shade would be cast on the rest of the border, and we know that bees prefer to visit plants that are growing in a sunny location. For this reason, and the fact that the shady conditions the tree would provide would necessarily alter our choice of plants, I have not incorporated a tree. There is still scope for a tree, however, as shady conditions could be overcome if the canopy of the tree were raised, for example.

Framework

Framework plants come in the shape of a shrub, and a climber trained up an obelisk; this will give some structure and height to the border and will compensate for the lack of a tree.

Flowers

The main planting material here consists of perennials which I have chosen to give some forage for bees and other pollinating insects from fairly early spring through to autumn. If, after they have finished flowering, and when the bees have had their fill, you deadhead the early flowering perennials, you will nearly always get another flush of blooms, albeit less robust, later in the season.

I have included *Agastache* 'Black Adder' in the plan because it is easy to get hold of, but it is worth pointing out that lots of new, exciting varieties of

Agastache are constantly being introduced, particularly from America. One that has caught my eye is called *A. rugosa* 'Honey' – surprise!

Fillers

Extra resources for bees can be provided by planting spring flowering bulbs, and other bulbs, and by filling in any gaps with annual plants.

Plant families

As we would expect, the majority of plants in this plan come from Primary families, with Secondary families coming close behind. Other families also make an appearance, adding to the overall form and texture of the border.

Ajuga reptens 'Atropurpurea' (13 – see page 38)

Key to the Large Traditional Border

Framework

Key reference	Plant	Units
C	*Clematis* 'Etoile Violette'	x 1
S	*Skimmia* x *confusa* 'Kew Green'	x 2

Flowers

	Plant	Units
1	*Lavandula angustifolia* 'Hidcote'	x 3
2	*Eryngium* x *tripartitum* 'Jade Frost'	x 3
3	*Echinacea purpurea*	x 3
4	*Agastache* 'Black Adder'	x 3
5	*Perovskia atriplicifolia* 'Little Spire'	x 3
6	*Aster* x *frikartii* 'Mönch'	x 3
7	*Pulmonaria* 'Beth's Pink'	x 3
8	*Achillea* 'Lilac Beauty'	x 3
9	*Geranium* 'Kashmir Pink'	x 3
10	*Polemonium caeruleum*	x 3
11	*Lamium maculatum* 'Orchid Frost'	x 4
12	*Verbascum* 'Cherry Helen'	x 3
13	*Ajuga reptens* 'Atropurpurea'	x 3
14	*Sedum* 'Brilliant'	x 3

Fillers

		Units
A	A mixture of the following to fill in gaps:	
	Heliotropium arborescens	x 12
	Nigella damascena	x 12
	Verbena bonariensis	x 12
B	A mixture of spring and summer flowering bulbs:	
	Allium 'Purple Sensation'	x 24
	Tulipa	x 36

(a mixture of Single Early, Triumph, and Single Late to cover from early spring to very early summer)

Plan for a Large Traditional Border
(numbers refer to key opposite)

I METRE

Sedum 'Brilliant' (14)

39

Skimmia x *confusa* 'Kew Green' (S)

Verbena bonariensis (A)

Echinacea purpurea (3)

Agastache 'Black Adder' (4)

Perovskia atriplicifolia 'Little Spire' (5)

Lamium maculatum 'Orchid Frost' (11)

Flowering times for the Large Traditional Border

	Evergreen	Spring	Summer	Autumn
Ajuga reptens 'Atropurpurea'	✓	✽		
Pulmonaria 'Beth's Pink'	✗	✽		
Skimmia x *confusa* 'Kew Green'	✓	✽		
Tulipa	✗	✽		
Lamium maculatum 'Orchid Frost'	✓	✽	✽	✽
Allium 'Purple Sensation'	✗		✽	
Eryngium x *tripartitum* 'Jade Frost'	✗		✽	
Geranium 'Kashmir Pink'	✗		✽	
Lavandula angustifolia 'Hidcote'	✓		✽	
Nigella damascena	✗		✽	
Polemonium caeruleum	✗		✽	
Verbascum 'Cherry Helen'	✗		✽	
Achillea 'Lilac Beauty'	✗		✽	✽
Agastache 'Black Adder'	✗		✽	✽
Clematis 'Etoile Violette'	✗		✽	✽
Heliotropium arborescens	✗		✽	✽
Perovskia atriplicifolia 'Little Spire'	✗		✽	✽
Verbena bonariensis	✗		✽	✽
Aster x frikartii 'Mönch'	✗			✽
Echinacea purpurea	✗			✽
Sedum 'Brilliant'	✗			✽

Small Traditional Border

Like the larger traditional border, this bed contains shrubs, perennials, bulbs and annuals – just not quite so many of them!

It is a fairly small space, some 2.5 metres by 2.5 metres, and the planting is quite dense; this means that the perennials will need dividing after a relatively short space of time.

Focus and framework

Because the space is limited, I have not included a focus plant, but framework plants are taken care of in the shape of an early flowering *Skimmia* and a rose, *Rosa* 'Nutkana', which has single, papery, pink blooms in the summer and carries beautiful red hips in the autumn.

Flowers

It was not easy choosing plants for this design; I really wanted to include more than was possible given the space restriction, and I had to be quite ruthless in my choice. Of paramount importance was that they had to be bee-friendly, and had a succession of flowering times, and only then could I select my favourites: needless to say, I had to leave out more than I put in!

Fillers

Tulips help augment the sources of pollen in the spring, while later in the bee season *Allium* come into their own. Here I have chosen the maroon-coloured *A. sphaerocephalon* and the white *A. ampeloprasum*, the latter being a veritable magnet for bees.

Left: Penstemon 'Blackberry Fancy' (1 – see page 44)

Key to the Small Traditional Border

Framework

Key reference	Plant	Units
R	*Rosa* 'Nutkana'	x 1
S	*Skimmia* x *confusa* 'Kew Green'	x 1

Flowers

1	*Penstemon* 'Blackberry Fancy'	x 3
2	*Aster* x *frikartii* 'Mönch'	x 3
3	*Agastache* 'Black Adder'	x 3
4	*Dahlia* 'Mermaid of Zennor'	x 3
5	*Echinacea purpurea*	x 3
6	*Ajuga reptens* 'Atropurpurea'	x 3
7	*Achillea* 'Apfelblüte'	x 3
8	*Lavandula angustifolia* 'Hidcote'	x 3
9	*Nepeta racemosa* 'Walker's Low'	x 3
10	*Geranium macrorrhizum* 'Ingwersen's Variety'	x 3
11	*Origanum laevigatum* 'Herrenhausen'	x 3

Fillers

A	A mixture of the following to fill in gaps:	
	Papaver somniferum	x 12
	Amberboa moschata	x 12
X	A mixture of spring and summer flowering bulbs:	
	Tulipa	x 30
	(a mixture of Single Early, Triumph, and Single Late to cover from early spring to very early summer)	
	Allium sphaerocephalon	x 15
	Allium ampeloprasum	x 15

Plan for a Small Traditional Border (numbers refer to key opposite)

Artist's impression of a Small Traditional Border

Echinacea purpurea (5)

Papaver somniferum (A)

Achillea 'Apfelblüte' (7)

Allium ampeloprasum (X)

Achillea 'Apfelblüte', *Lavandula angustifolia* 'Hidcote', and *Nepeta racemosa* 'Walker's Low' (7, 8, 9)

Flowering times for the Small Traditional Border

	Evergreen	Spring	Summer	Autumn
Ajuga reptens 'Atropurpurea'	✓	❀		
Tulipa	✗	❀		
Skimmia x *confusa* 'Kew Green'	✓	❀		
Geranium macrorrhizum 'Ingwersen's Variety'	✓	❀	❀	
Allium ampeloprasum	✗		❀	
Allium sphaerocephalon	✗		❀	
Lavandula angustifolia 'Hidcote'	✓		❀	
Nepeta racemosa 'Walker's Low'	✗		❀	
Origanum laevigatum 'Herrenhausen'	✓		❀	
Papaver somniferum	✗		❀	
Rosa 'Nutkana'	✗		❀	
Achillea 'Apfelblüte'	✗		❀	❀
Agastache 'Black Adder'	✗		❀	❀
Amberboa moschata	✗		❀	❀
Penstemon 'Blackberry Fancy'	✗		❀	❀
Aster x *frikartii* 'Mönch'	✗			❀
Dahlia 'Mermaid of Zennor'	✗			❀
Echinacea purpurea	✗			❀

Cottage Garden Plans

It is probably as well to point out that the image of the garden with roses around the door and hollyhocks emerging from a profusion of sweet Williams growing against the stone wall of the pristine thatched cottage, complete with rosy-cheeked, bonneted girl lovingly watering her pots of pelargoniums, is just that – an image, not a reality. Helen Leach, in her book *Cultivating Myths* (see Further Reading), looks at the history and development of the 'cottage garden' and puts the concept squarely in the realm of fiction. She argues that is there is no 'authentic' cottage garden – and never has been – and, given the evidence, I am inclined to agree.

Her theory does not, however, detract from the fact that a particular *style* of garden has evolved over the years that many of us recognize as a 'cottage garden'. Indeed, Leach rounds off her argument by saying, 'The true cottage garden does not consist of particular plants, but of any fruit, flower or vegetable that has a constitution suited to your particular locality.' And it is the *combination* of fruit, flower or vegetable, artfully arranged and mingled, that to my mind is the thing that sets a cottage garden apart from any other type of garden. In addition, the type of garden that might be designated 'cottage' is, in effect, disorganized formality. By this I mean that plants – especially ornamentals – are often arranged in quite an *ad hoc* way, but are nevertheless constrained within strict boundaries. This can lead to a dishevelled veneer; but look behind the chaos and you will see walls, hedges and paths creating definite boundaries.

So, myths and theories aside, I have put together two versions of my vision of a cottage garden border, complete with fruit, flowers and herbs. (They do not include vegetables, which I have reserved for another design.) The first is for a large border, and the second for an 'island' bed.

Large Cottage Garden Border

This plan is for a fairly large border, 6 metres by 2 metres in size, which backs on to a wall against which espaliered apples can be trained. Alternatively, the apples could be trained along wires, supported by stout posts, to form a division in the garden, as demonstrated in the Beekeeper's Garden (see page 158).

Focus

A word about apple varieties first. A couple of things are useful to bear in mind when choosing which ones to grow. First, find out which varieties are best suited to where you live: some will struggle in colder, wetter parts of the country. Second, in order to ensure effective pollination, the varieties you choose have to be in the same pollination group as each other, or at a push, one group removed. Third, you need to decide whether you want a culinary or a dessert apple, or one that doubles up as both. Fourth, find out what rootstock the apple has been grafted on to: the more vigorous the rootstock, the larger the tree, so some rootstocks are not suitable for training into espaliers. And fifth, choose varieties that you know you will like!

If all this sounds complicated, have a look at the website of the National Fruit Collection in Kent, or one of the specialist fruit growers (see Useful Addresses and Websites), where you will find lots of information and advice.

I have chosen two varieties, 'Cox's Orange Pippin' and 'James Grieve', both of which are available already part-trained as espaliers and are therefore on a suitable rootstock, and are of the same pollination group. Planted in the open, they might struggle a little in the north-west of England where I live, but if they are trained against a wall that will provide shelter and a modicum of warmth, they should be fine.

Framework

There are any number of shrubs that I could have included in this plan, but whenever I think of 'cottage garden', roses spring to mind. The one I have chosen, 'Jaquenetta', is an English rose, bred by David Austin, which is described as having single flowers, although some of them may be semi-double; either way, the stamens are accessible by visiting bees! It has pale pink verging on apricot flowers, which I think will sit very nicely among the pinks, purples and apricots of the summer and autumn blooms.

Flowers

Mixed in with some typical cottage perennials like *Geranium*, *Alcea* (hollyhock) and *Helenium* are herbs that can either be used in the kitchen or left to flower for the bees – or both.

Fillers

As well as tulips to carry the border through spring into summer, I have dotted chives (*Allium schoenoprasum*) in the gaps and alpine strawberries (*Fragaria vesca*) between the stepping stones in front of the apple trees. Alpine strawberries seem to flower and fruit for ever and if you have a big enough harvest, they make a luxurious and unbelievably delicious addition to home-made strawberry jam.

Plant families

As always, Primary families, Asteraceae and Lamiaceae, feature strongly in this plan. Some Secondary families (Rosaceae and Scrophulariaceae) make an appearance, with a couple of specimens from Other families.

1 METRE

Plan for a Large Cottage Garden Border (numbers refer to key opposite)

Key to the Large Cottage Garden Border

Focus and framework

Key reference	Plant	Units
M	*Malus domestica*, trained as espaliers on wall:	
	Malus 'Cox's Orange Pippin'	x 1
	Malus 'James Grieve'	x 1
R	*Rosa* 'Jaquenetta'	x 1

Flowers

1	*Achillea* 'Terracotta'	x 3
2	*Rosmarinus officinalis*	x 3
3	*Papaver orientale* 'Bolero'	x 3
4	*Agastache* 'Black Adder'	x 2
5	*Alcea ficifolia*	x 3
6	*Nepeta racemosa* 'Walker's Low'	x 3
7	*Lavandula angustifolia* 'Hidcote'	x 3
8	*Lavandula angustifolia* 'Hidcote'	x 3
9	*Salvia officinalis* 'Icterina'	x 4
10	*Aster* x *frikartii* 'Mönch'	x 3
11	*Origanum vulgare*	x 4
12	*Helenium* 'Moerheim Beauty'	x 3
13	*Salvia officinalis* Purpurascens Group	x 3
14	*Doronicum* 'Miss Mason'	x 3
15	*Echinacea purpurea* 'White Swan'	x 3
16	*Geranium sanguineum* 'Elke'	x 3

Fillers

X	*Tulipa*	x 30
	(a mixture of Single Early, Triumph, and Single Late to cover from early spring to very early summer)	
A	*Allium schoenoprasum*	x 8
F	*Fragaria vesca*	x 11

Achillea 'Terracotta' and *Lavandula angustifolia* 'Hidcote' (1, 8)

Malus domestica trained as an espalier (M)

Geranium sanguineum 'Elke' (16)

Malus domestica (M)

Salvia officinalis 'Icterina' (9)

Helenium 'Moerheim Beauty' (12)

Origanum vulgare (11)

Allium schoenoprasum (A)

Alcea ficifolia (5)

Flowering times of the Large Cottage Garden Border

	Evergreen	Spring	Summer	Autumn
Doronicum 'Miss Mason'	✗	❀		
Malus domestica	✗	❀		
Rosmarinus officinalis	✓	❀		
Tulipa	✗	❀		
Fragaria vesca	✗	❀	❀	
Alcea ficifolia	✗		❀	
Lavandula angustifolia 'Hidcote'	✓		❀	
Papaver orientale 'Bolero'	✗		❀	
Origanum vulgare	✓		❀	
Salvia officinalis Purpurascens Group	✓		❀	
Achillea 'Terracotta'	✗		❀	❀
Agastache 'Black Adder'	✗		❀	❀
Allium schoenoprasum	✗		❀	❀
Geranium sanguineum 'Elke'	✗		❀	❀
Nepeta racemosa 'Walker's Low'	✗		❀	❀
Rosa 'Jaquenetta'	✗		❀	❀
Aster x *frikartii* 'Mönch'	✗			❀
Echinacea purpurea 'White Swan'	✗			❀
Helenium 'Moerheim Beauty'	✗			❀
Salvia officinalis 'Icterina'	✓			

Cottage Garden Island Bed

This cottage garden plan is for an 'island' bed, measuring some 5 metres by 5.5 metres. It is more formal in its layout than the larger plan, and could be adapted to include vegetables if desired.

Focus

At the heart of the plot is an apple, *Malus* 'Reverend W. Wilks', trained as a goblet. This variety is ideal for such manipulation. Being self-fertile, it will produce a good crop in the absence of another tree for pollination, although there will be a more uniform crop if there is an additional one close by.

Framework

The main framework in this garden is provided by the low outline hedge of *Buxus sempervirens* 'Suffruticosa'. This has a compact, very dense form, with small leaves, and is ideal as an edging plant.

Flowers

This is really a garden of flowers, with lots of 'old-fashioned' plants like *Lavandula, Aster, Sedum* and *Geranium*, which between them provide colour for us and food for bees throughout the season.

Fillers

I have suggested planting thyme between the stepping stones leading to the apple tree. The thyme will soften the edges of the stones, and if you step on its leaves they will release their oil and you will be greeted by a spicy aroma.

Crocus and *Allium schoenoprasum* (chives) are planted either side of the stones, while *Allium, Tulipa*, annual *Papaver* (poppy) and *Phacelia* fill in the gaps in the main planting. If you allow the latter two to self-seed they will form a tapestry of unifying colour during the following years. A little judicious thinning may be called for each spring, however, as they can be prolific self-seeders and will take over the plot if you allow them to.

Plant families

Once again, the Primary families feature strongly. In this plan Other families outnumber the Secondary families, but all the plants are good for bees, so this doesn't matter.

Phacelia tanacetifolia (P – see page 59)

Key to the Cottage Garden Island Bed

Focus

Key reference	Plant	Units
A	*Malus domestica* 'Reverend W. Wilks' (apple), trained as a goblet	x 1

Framework

	Buxus sempervirens 'Suffruticosa' (hedging)	x 150

Flowers

1	*Nepeta hybrida* 'Pink Candy'	x 3
2	*Lavandula angustifolia* 'Hidcote'	x 3
3	*Eryngium* x *tripartitum* 'Jade Frost'	x 3
4	*Digitalis purpurea* 'Pam's Choice'	x 3
5	*Pulmonaria* 'Cotton Cool'	x 3
6	*Sedum* 'Strawberries and Cream'	x 3
7	*Geranium pratense* var. *striatum* 'Splish Splash'	x 3
8	*Echinacea purpurea*	x 3
9	*Polemonium caeruleum*	x 3
10	*Aster* x *frikartii* 'Mönch'	x 3
11	*Verbascum* 'Cherry Helen'	x 3
12	*Rosmarinus officinalis*	x 3
13	*Salvia officinalis* Purpurascens Group with	x 3
	Satureja montana	x 5
14	*Hyssopus officinalis* (pink variety) with	x 3
	Origanum vulgare	x 5
15	*Hyssopus officinalis* (blue variety) with	x 3
	Origanum vulgare	x 5
16	*Salvia officinalis* with	x 3
	Satureja montana	x 5

Fillers

C	*Allium schoenoprasum*	x 24
	(planted alongside stepping stones)	
H	*Thymus vulgaris*	x 18
	(planted between stepping stones)	
O	*Allium* 'Purple Sensation'	x 20
	(planted in gaps)	
P	*Phacelia tanacetifolia*	x 20
	(planted in gaps)	
R	*Crocus chrysanthus* 'Cream Beauty'	x 40
	and *Crocus vernus* 'Remembrance'	x 40
	(planted alongside stepping stones)	
T	*Tulipa* 'Purissima'	x 24
	and *Tulipa* 'Negrita'	x 24
	(planted in gaps)	
V	*Papaver somniferum*	x 20
	(planted in gaps)	

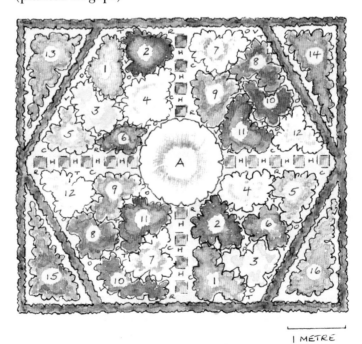

1 METRE

Plan for a Cottage Garden Island Bed (numbers refer to key opposite and above)

Malus domestica, showing goblet training (A)

Geranium pratense var. *striatum* 'Splish Splash' (7)

Pulmonaria 'Cotton Cool' (5)

Sedum 'Strawberries and Cream' (6)

Digitalis purpurea 'Pam's Choice' (4)

Papaver somniferum (V)

Flowering times of the Cottage Garden Island Bed

	Evergreen	Spring	Summer	Autumn
Crocus sp	✗	❁		
Malus domestica 'Reverend W. Wilks'	✗	❁		
Pulmonaria 'Cotton Cool'	✓	❁		
Rosmarinus officinalis	✓	❁		
Tulipa sp	✗	❁		
Allium 'Purple Sensation'	✗		❁	
Digitalis purpurea 'Pam's Choice'	✗		❁	
Eryngium x *tripartitum* 'Jade Frost'	✗		❁	
Hyssopus officinalis	✓		❁	
Lavandula angustifolia 'Hidcote'	✓		❁	
Origanum vulgare	✓		❁	
Papaver somniferum	✗		❁	
Phacelia tanacetifolia	✗		❁	
Salvia officinalis	✓		❁	
Satureja montana	✓		❁	
Thymus vulgaris	✓		❁	
Verbascum 'Cherry Helen'	✗		❁	
Allium schoenoprasum	✗		❁	❁
Geranium pratense var. *striatum* 'Splish Splash'	✗		❁	❁
Nepeta hybrida 'Pink Candy'	✗		❁	❁
Polemonium caeruleum	✗		❁	❁
Aster x *frikartii* 'Mönch'	✗			❁
Echinacea purpurea	✗			❁
Sedum 'Strawberries and Cream'	✗			❁
Buxus sempervirens 'Suffruticosa'	✓			

Designer Border

I debated with myself as to whether this should be called a 'Designer' border, since all borders are, to some degree, designed! I have, however, employed some of the designer's 'tools' more blatantly in this border than in the others, so I have persuaded myself that I can give it this somewhat grandiose name.

First, the way that I have divided the area up into segments relies on the premise of the Golden Ratio, which centres on the number 1.618. This number, denoted by the Greek letter 'phi' (Ø), comes about if you divide a line into two parts so that the longer part divided by the smaller part is also equal to the whole length divided by the longer part. It has long been held that a rectangle whose sides are in the ratio of 1 to Ø has the most pleasing proportions. In my design I have approximated the figure to 1.6, so all my rectangles have the ratio of 1 to 1.6.

Second, I have noticeably employed a number of the principles of design that we looked at in Chapter 2, especially balance, focalization and repetition. In order to do this I have deliberately chosen a modest palette of colours, and used form and texture quite consciously to create what I hope is a pleasing combination of plants which are brought together in a contemporary way.

The overall effect that I hope to achieve is a 'tapestry' of recurring individual plants, which is why I have restricted the number of different varieties to only five. The tapestry is interspersed with blocks of colour (the *Lavandula*) and punctuated by the standard *Rosa* which also give height. Running through the 'tapestry' there is a unifying thread in the form of *Tulipa* in the spring and *Allium* and *Verbena* later in the season.

The plan is for a space some 4.8 metres by 5 metres; because it is formed of rectangles, however, it could easily be adjusted to fit a smaller or larger space by adding or subtracting rows of rectangles.

Focus and framework

The focal points are centred on the standard roses, *Rosa* 'Kew Gardens', which have small, single white flowers and are covered in lovely red hips in the autumn. The block planting of *Lavandula* also gives year-round structure to the planting.

Flowers and fillers

Despite not having used many different perennials, the ones that I have chosen provide interest for us and food for bees throughout summer and autumn, with *Tulipa* starting the season in spring.

Plant families

As always, the Primary families make up the major part of the planting, with representatives from the Secondary and Other families also cropping up here and there.

Geranium sanguineum 'Elke' (2 – see page 64)

Key to the Designer Border

Framework

Key reference	Plant	Units
R	*Rosa* 'Kew Gardens' (standard)	x 4

Flowers

1	*Lavandula angustifolia* 'Hidcote'	x 18
2	*Geranium sanguineum* 'Elke'	x 16
3	*Echinacea purpurea* 'Primadonna White'	x 16
4	*Nepeta racemosa* 'Walker's Low'	x 16
5	*Salvia nemerosa* 'Amethyst'	x 8
6	*Eryngium bourgatii* 'Picos Amethyst'	x 8

Fillers

X	A mixture of:	
	Allium 'Purple Sensation'	x 21
	Tulipa 'Purissima' and 'Negrita'	x 63
	Verbena bonariensis	x 21

Allium 'Purple Sensation' (X)

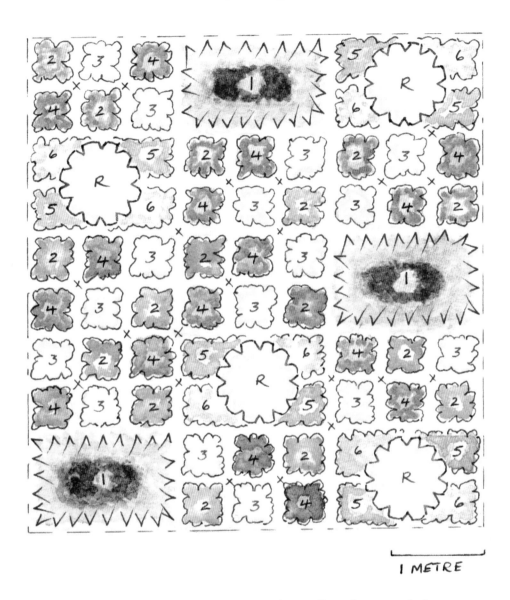

1 METRE

Plan for a Designer Border(numbers refer to key opposite)

Echinacea purpurea 'Primadonna White' (3)

Eryngium bourgatii 'Picos Amethyst' (6)

Nepeta racemosa 'Walker's Low' (4)

Salvia nemerosa 'Amethyst' (5)

Flowering times of the Designer Border

	Evergreen	Spring	Summer	Autumn
Tulipa 'Purissima' and 'Negrita'	✗	❀		
Allium 'Purple Sensation'	✗		❀	
Lavandula angustifolia 'Hidcote'	✓		❀	
Echinacea purpurea 'Primadonna White'	✗		❀	❀
Eryngium bourgatii 'Picos Amethyst'	✗		❀	❀
Geranium sanguineum 'Elke'	✗		❀	❀
Nepeta racemosa 'Walker's Low'	✗		❀	❀
Rosa 'Kew Gardens'	✗		❀	❀
Salvia nemerosa 'Amethyst'	✗		❀	❀
Verbena bonariensis	✗		❀	❀

Native Naturalistic Border

This plan features only native (or near-native) plants. I have included this in order to show that you can have an area containing 'wild' flowers that doesn't have to be a meadow. The plants may not be as well behaved as their cultivated counterparts, being more lax in their habit and with a tendency to seed themselves given the chance, but they are nonetheless attractive in their own way and are beloved by bees.

The plan is for a fairly modest space, covering an area some 2 metres by 2.5 metres. If you have a larger area to fill then it is easy to repeat the whole or part of the plan accordingly.

Focus and framework

Since the space is small, I have not included a focus or even any framework plants. If you have a larger area and want to include a focal point, I think I would choose *Malus sylvestris* – the native crab apple – for its white blossom in the spring and fruits in the autumn.

Flowers and fillers

This plan consists almost entirely of flowers which bloom mainly during the summer months. This could be regarded as falling short of the aim of providing a suitable source of food for bees for as long a period as possible, but I feel certain that you would probably not want to surrender your entire garden to this type of planting, so there are bound to be flowers available elsewhere in the garden to cover the spring period. If, however, you wanted to include a really good bee plant that flowers for an incredibly long period then you could do no worse than *Taraxacum officinale* (dandelion). The main problem with this plant is that it is very difficult to get rid of once you have it, and it will seed itself in places you didn't know it was possible for anything to grow!

Plant families

Unusually, the Other families outnumber Primary families in this plan so we are drawing on a much more diverse collection of plants. All, however, are bee-friendly, so we can bend our rules a little now and then.

Cicorium intybus (2 – see page 70)

Key to the Native Naturalistic Border

Flowers

Key reference	Plant	Units
1	*Verbascum nigrum*	x 3
2	*Cicorium intybus*	x 3
3	*Scabiosa columbaria*	x 3
4	*Achillea ptarmica*	x 3
5	*Origanum vulgare*	x 5
6	*Digitalis purpurea*	x 3
7	*Campanula glomerata*	x 3
8	*Limonium binervosum*	x 3
9	*Centaurea scabiosa*	x 3
10	*Geranium pratense*	x 3

Fillers

X	*Ornithogalum pyrenaicum*	x 30

An artist's impression of a Native Naturalistic Border

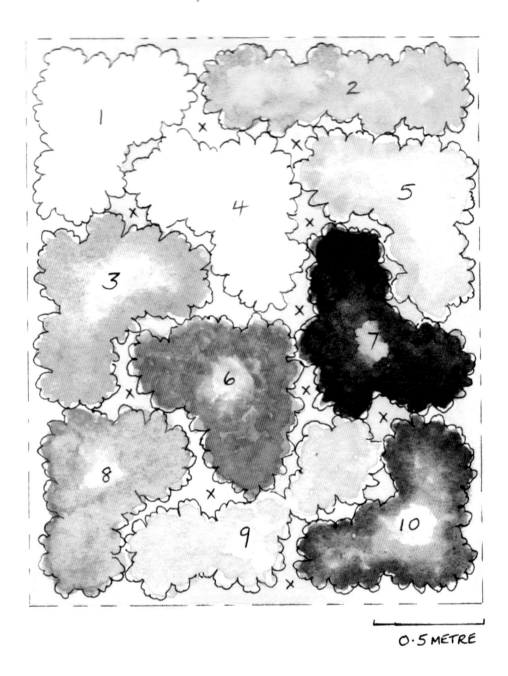

0·5 METRE

Plan for a Native Naturalistic Border (numbers refer to key opposite)

Scabiosa columbaria (3)

Geranium pratense (10)

Digitalis purpurea (6)

Limonium binervosum (8)

Flowering times of the
Native Naturalistic Border

	Evergreen	Spring	Summer	Autumn
Achillea ptarmica	✗		✶	
Campanula glomerata	✗		✶	
Digitalis purpurea	✗		✶	
Geranium pratense	✗		✶	
Limonium binervosum	✗		✶	
Origanum vulgare	✗		✶	
Ornithogalum pyrenaicum	✗		✶	
Scabiosa columbaria	✗		✶	
Centaurea scabiosa	✗		✶	✶
Cicorium intybus	✗		✶	✶
Verbascum nigrum	✗		✶	✶

Cultivated Naturalistic Border

This border takes part of its inspiration from native species that have been developed into more 'garden-worthy' specimens: this approach accounts for some of the plants, like *Verbascum, Geranium* and *Achillea*. I have included other plants because, to my mind, they integrate well into the overall theme and add interest through either their form or their colour: *Kniphofia* and *Allium* are examples of this.

I have also been inspired by the so-called New Perennial style – sometimes called 'prairie' planting – which, as its name implies, relies heavily on perennial plants rather than on trees and shrubs to give both form and structure. Usually included in 'prairie' planting are grasses, but I have not used them in this plan. Grasses do add another dimension to the planting, but because they are wind-pollinated they are worthless to bees, and I would rather use the space for a plant that is of benefit to our buzzy friends.

This plan is for a bed 6 metres by 2 metres and the plants have been arranged in smaller blocks than in other plans, to give a fragmented effect, although each variety could easily be grouped together in larger numbers to give more solid areas of planting – the choice is yours.

Focus and framework

Focus and framework plants don't feature in this plan at all; instead it relies on the overall arrangement of the flowers to give it form.

Flowers

In this plan, there is something in flower from mid-spring through to autumn and the first frosts, so the bees are fairly well catered for. Many of these flowers also 'die' well, in that if you don't cut them back in autumn they will provide interesting silhouettes and shapes in the winter months, especially during periods of heavy frost. Many of the seed heads will also afford food for birds during the winter.

Fillers

Early flowering infill is offered by *Camassia*, followed by two kinds of *Allium*, the self-explanatory 'Purple Sensation' and a beautiful white form with scented, lace-like flowers, *A. neapolitanum* Cowanii Group, later in the season.

Plant families

Primary families don't feature as much as you might expect in this collection, although they still have a presence. Single representatives from families in the Other section together outnumber Primary and Secondary family members, which doesn't fit our blueprint; but they are all bee-friendly.

Scabiosa columbaria subsp *ochroleuca* 'Moon Dance' (8 – see page 76)

Key to the Cultivated Naturalistic Border

Flowers

Key reference	Plant	Units
1	*Cirsium rivulare* 'Atropurpureum'	x 3
2	*Geranium macrorrhizum* 'Ingwersen's Variety'	x 3
3	*Verbascum* 'Sierra Sunset'	x 4
4	*Papaver orientale* 'Bolero'	3
5	*Veronica longifolia*	x 4
6	*Echinacea purpurea* 'Primadonna White'	x 3
7	*Achillea* 'Martina'	x 3
8	*Scabiosa columbaria* subsp *ochroleuca* 'Moon Dance'	x 5
9	*Agastache* 'Black Adder'	x 3
10	*Sidalcea* 'Elsie Heugh'	x 3
11	*Monarda fistulosa*	x 4
12	*Kniphofia* 'Toffee Nosed'	x 3

Fillers

A	*Allium* 'Purple Sensation'	x 18
B	*Allium neapolitanum* Cowanii Group	x 12
C	*Camassia leichtlinii*	x 12

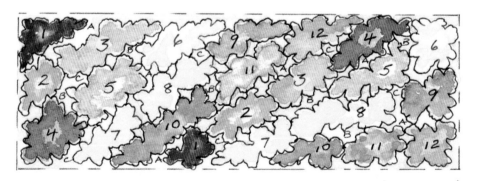

1 METRE

Plan for a Cultivated Naturalistic Border

Cirsium rivulare 'Atropurpureum' (1)

Veronica longifolia (5)

Echinacea purpurea 'Primadonna White' (6)

Achillea 'Martina' (7)

Agastache 'Black Adder' (9)

Sidalcea 'Elsie Heugh' (10)

Flowering times of the Cultivated Naturalistic Border

	Evergreen	Spring	Summer	Autumn
Camassia leichtlinii	✗	❀		
Geranium macrorrhizum 'Ingwersen's Variety'	✓	❀	❀	
Achillea 'Martina'	✗		❀	
Allium neapolitanum Cowanii Group	✗		❀	
Allium 'Purple Sensation'	✗		❀	
Cirsium rivulare 'Atropurpureum'	✗		❀	
Monarda fistulosa	✗		❀	
Papaver orientale 'Bolero'	✗		❀	
Sidalcea 'Elsie Heugh'	✗		❀	
Verbascum 'Sierra Sunset'	✗		❀	
Agastache 'Black Adder'	✗		❀	❀
Kniphofia 'Toffee Nosed'	✗		❀	❀
Scabiosa columbaria subsp *ochroleuca* 'Moon Dance'	✗		❀	❀
Veronica longifolia	✗		❀	❀
Echinacea purpurea 'Primadonna White'	✗			❀

Left: Kniphofia 'Toffee Nosed' (12 – see page 76)

Combination Naturalistic Border

This plan, as its title suggests, is a combination of plants taken from the Native and Cultivated Borders, above. Cultivated varieties are in the majority, however, because I envisage this plan being incorporated more readily into an existing garden than the straightforward Native Naturalistic Border.

This plan is for a bed 2.5 metres by 2.5 metres in size but it can easily be duplicated to fill a larger space if desired.

Focus and framework

Because the area is relatively small, focus and framework plants don't feature in this plan at all, but, as with the Native Naturalistic Border, you could incorporate a crab apple, *Malus sylvestris*, if you have a larger area.

Flowers

I would wager that some people would be hard pushed to distinguish the native specimens from the 'garden' ones in this plan: I think it is particularly true of *Geranium pratense*, whose violet-blue flowers are every bit as good as some of its cultivated cousins.

Fillers

Having seen *Camassia* dotted through a managed flower meadow I couldn't resist following suit: their presence gives an almost regal air to the area at the end of spring before the infill baton is taken over by *Allium* 'Purple Sensation'.

Plant families

Primary and Secondary families, beloved by bees, are the mainstay of this collection, although a number of plants from Other families are also included.

Right: Camassia leichtlinii (X – see page 82)

Key to the Combination Naturalistic Border

Flowers

Key reference	Plant	Units
1	*Geranium pratense*	x 3
2	*Echinacea purpurea* 'Primadonna White'	x 3
3	*Scabiosa columbaria* subsp *ochroleuca* 'Moon Dance'	x 3
4	*Veronica longifolia*	x 3
5	*Verbascum* 'Sierra Sunset'	x 3
6	*Centaurea scabiosa*	x 3
7	*Digitalis purpurea*	x 3
8	*Campanula glomerata*	x 3
9	*Achillea* 'Martina'	x 3
10	*Geranium macrorrhizum* 'Ingwersen's Variety'	x 3
11	*Monarda fistulosa*	x 3
12	*Agastache* 'Black Adder'	x 3

Fillers

X	*Allium* 'Purple Sensation'	x 30
	Camassia leichtlinii	x 15

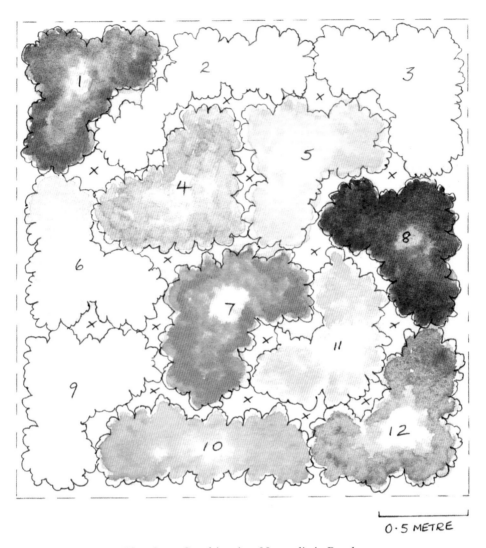

Plan for a Combination Naturalistic Border

Left: Allium 'Purple Sensation' (X – see key opposite)

Geranium pratense (1)

Campanula glomerata (8)

Veronica longifolia (4)

Digitalis purpurea (7)

Flowering times of the Combination Naturalistic Border

	Evergreen	Spring	Summer	Autumn
Camassia leichtlinii	✗	❀		
Geranium macrorrhizum 'Ingwersen's Variety'	✓	❀	❀	
Achillea 'Martina'	✗		❀	
Allium 'Purple Sensation'	✗		❀	
Monarda fistulosa	✗		❀	
Campanula glomerata	✗		❀	
Digitalis purpurea	✗		❀	
Geranium pratense	✗		❀	
Verbascum 'Sierra Sunset'	✗		❀	
Agastache 'Black Adder'	✗		❀	❀
Centaurea scabiosa	✗		❀	❀
Scabiosa columbaria subsp *ochroleuca* 'Moon Dance'	✗		❀	❀
Veronica longifolia	✗		❀	❀
Echinacea purpurea 'Primadonna White'	✗			❀

Shrub Border

There may be a spot in your garden that you would like to plant up with shrubs. This is certainly an option if you have the room, or if you want a fairly low-maintenance area. Shrubs are pretty undemanding when it comes to care, although they may require some feeding to keep them up to scratch, and some will need pruning to encourage them to produce flowers and continue looking good. But for the most part they require relatively little attention. A number of shrubs are good bee plants, too, providing a succession of forage from spring through to autumn.

This plan covers an area of 5 metres by 5 metres, which is a comparatively large space.

Focus, framework and flowers

You could say that this plan is made up entirely of framework plants, since they are all shrubs and the overall framework is present throughout the year. This could potentially be a lacklustre prospect but I have tried to alleviate this by incorporating a mixture of both evergreen and deciduous specimens, with foliage of different textures and a variety of flower colour that takes us from spring right through to autumn. In this way some of the shrubs, especially the *Lavandula*, take on the role of flowers.

Fillers

I have suggested underplanting the shrubs with *Anemone nemerosa*, a spring flowering rhizome that will tolerate the shady conditions presented by the shrubs.

Plant families

This being a border of shrubs, it is not surprising that Primary families do not feature heavily, since most of Asteraceae and Lamiaceae are herbaceous plants. Even though the majority of plants belong to Other families, they are bee-friendly.

Hebe 'Autumn Glory' (H – see page 88)

Key to the Shrub Border

Flowers

Key reference	Plant	Units
A	*Hydrangea aspera* subsp *sargentiana*	x 1
B	*Buddleja* x *weyeriana* 'Sungold'	x 1
C	*Caryopteris* x *clandonensis* 'Grand Bleu'	x 4
H	*Hebe* 'Autumn Glory'	x 6
K	*Skimmia* x *confusa* 'Kew Green'	x 2
L	*Lavandula angustifolia* 'Hidcote'	x 12
M	*Mahonia aquifolium*	x 2
O	*Cotoneaster harrovianus*	x 2
R	*Rosa* 'Windrush'	x 3
S	*Salix hastata* 'Wehrhahnii'	x 2
V	*Viburnum tinus* 'Eve Price'	x 1
X	A mixture of *Anemone nemerosa*:	x 90
	Anemone nemerosa 'Alba'	
	Anemone nemerosa 'Allenii'	
	Anemone nemerosa 'Pentre Pink'	

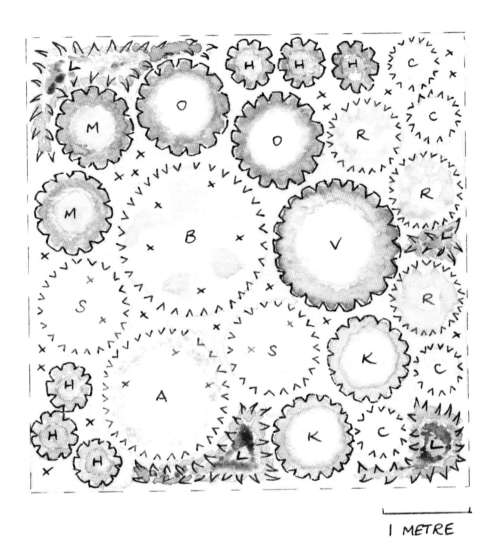

Plan for a Shrub Border

Left: Skimmia x *confusa* 'Kew Green' (K)

Hydrangea aspera subsp *sargentiana* (A)

Caryopteris x *clandonensis* 'Grand Bleu' (C)

Mahonia aquifolium (M)

Viburnum tinus 'Eve Price' (V)

Flowering times of the Shrub Border

	Evergreen	Spring	Summer	Autumn
Anemone nemerosa 'Alba'	✗	✸		
Anemone nemerosa 'Allenii'	✗	✸		
Anemone nemerosa 'Pentre Pink'	✗	✸		
Mahonia aquifolium	✓	✸		
Salix hastata 'Wehrhahnii'	✗	✸		
Skimmia x *confusa* 'Kew Green'	✓	✸		
Viburnum tinus 'Eve Price'	✓	✸		
Cotoneaster harrovianus	✓		✸	
Lavandula angustifolia 'Hidcote'	✓		✸	
Buddleja x *weyeriana* 'Sungold'	✗		✸	✸
Caryopteris x *clandonensis* 'Grand Bleu'	✗		✸	✸
Hebe 'Autumn Glory'	✓		✸	✸
Hydrangea aspera subsp *sargentiana*	✗		✸	✸
Rosa 'Windrush'	✗		✸	✸

Colour Themes

In this section there are three plans: one containing blue and yellow flowers; one with red and yellow flowers; and a larger 'rainbow' border which includes – yes, you've guessed! – flowers which just about cover all the colours of the rainbow.

Above: Mahonia aquifolium (A – see page 96)
Left: Doronicum x *excelsum* 'Harpur Crewe' (10 – see page 96)

Blue and Yellow Border

We are certainly on safe ground with blue and yellow when it comes to colour in 'bee plants'. These two colours are easily detected by bees, since they fall well within their visual spectrum. This combination of colours is also pleasing to the human eye; the selection in this design especially so, with 'blue' plants at the purple end of blue complementing the buttery-yellow selection of plants beautifully.

The plan is for a fairly modest space, some 2.5 metres by 2.5 metres. If you have a larger area to fill then it is easy to repeat the whole or part of the plan accordingly.

Focus and framework

Since the area is quite small I have not included a focus plant. The framework plant, *Mahonia,* may not be at the top of everyone's favourite shrub list, but it is an ideal bee plant and is evergreen to boot.

Flowers and fillers

As always, flowers are the major type of plant in the scheme and cover the main foraging period for bees; spring and early summer colour is also supplied by tulips and *Crocus,* which bring a fillip of much-needed colour to the border. *Crocus,* in particular, provide bees with an early source of food.

Plant families

The majority of the plants fall into the Primary families, with two from the Secondary ones and a smattering of Others, so we can be sure that they will all be both bee-friendly and give us a pleasing arrangement of form and texture.

Right: Salvia x *sylvestris* 'Blauhügel' (5– see page 96)

Key to the Blue and Yellow Border

Framework

Key reference	Plant	Units
A	*Mahonia aquifolium*	x 1

Flowers

1	*Perovskia atriplicifolia* 'Little Spire'	x 3
2	*Echinacea purpurea* 'Harvest Moon'	x 3
3	*Echinops ritro* 'Veitch's Blue'	x 3
4	*Kniphofia* 'Bees' Sunset'	x 3
5	*Salvia* x *sylvestris* 'Blauhügel'	x 3
6	*Verbascum* 'Sierra Sunset'	x 3
7	*Achillea* 'Martina'	x 3
8	*Helenium* 'Gartensonne'	x 3
9	*Polemonium* 'Bressingham Purple'	x 3
10	*Doronicum* x *excelsum* 'Harpur Crewe'	x 3
11	*Veronica longifolia* 'Blue John'	x 3

Fillers

B	A mixture to fill in gaps:	
	Centaurea cyanus	x 24
	Helianthus annuus 'Garden Statement'	x 6
X	A mixture of spring and summer flowering bulbs:	x 45
	Tulipa	

(a mixture of yellow Single Early, Triumph, and Single Late to cover from early spring to very early summer)
Crocus (yellow and purple varieties)
Allium caeruleum

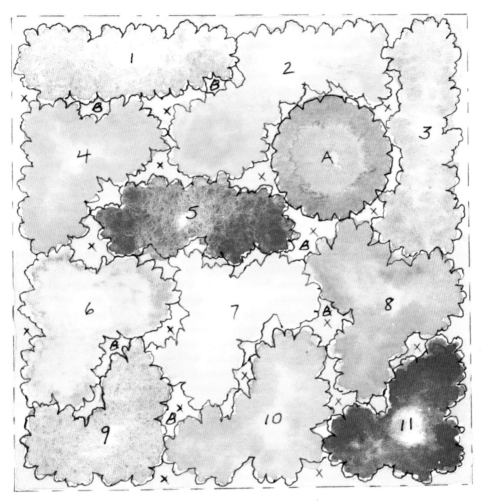

Plan for a Blue and Yellow Border

0·5 METRE

Helenium 'Gartensonne' (8)

Echinacea purpurea 'Harvest Moon' (2)

Achillea 'Martina' (7)

Echinops ritro 'Veitch's Blue' (3)

Polemonium 'Bressingham Purple' (9)

Flowering times of the Blue and Yellow Border

	Evergreen	Spring	Summer	Autumn
Crocus	✗	❀		
Doronicum x *excelsum* 'Harpur Crewe'	✗	❀		
Mahonia aquifolium	✓	❀		
Tulipa	✗	❀		
Achillea 'Martina'	✗		❀	
Allium caeruleum	✗		❀	
Centaurea cyanus	✗		❀	
Echinops ritro 'Veitch's Blue'	✗		❀	
Salvia x *sylvestris* 'Blauhügel'	✗		❀	
Helenium 'Gartensonne'	✗		❀	❀
Helianthus annuus 'Garden Statement'	✗		❀	❀
Kniphofia 'Bees' Sunset'	✗		❀	❀
Polemonium 'Bressingham Purple'	✗		❀	❀
Verbascum 'Sierra Sunset'	✗		❀	❀
Veronica longifolia 'Blue John'	✗		❀	❀
Echinacea purpurea 'Harvest Moon'	✗			❀
Perovskia atriplicifolia 'Little Spire'	✗			❀

Red and Yellow Border

We know that red falls outside the spectrum of colour that can be detected by bees, so you may be wondering why I have included a plan for a hot, red, orange and yellow border. It is really because bees can detect yellow that makes this colour combination possible. Also, despite its colour, bees are attracted to the *Monarda* (or to give it its common name, bee balm) for the abundant nectar, and the red rose has bright yellow stamens which the bee identifies.

The plan is for a smallish space, some 2.5 metres by 2.5 metres, but it can be extended if you have a larger area to fill.

Focus and framework

I have not included a focus plant in this quite small area, although you could argue that the framework plant – a rose – is rather special in its own right. *Rosa* 'Rose of Picardy' is a single, red-flowered rose from David Austin which has beautiful hips in the autumn.

Flowers and fillers

Flowers form the major part of the design, and as usual I have tried to include plants to cover the foraging season of the bees. In this part of the colour wheel spring flowering plants that are good for bees are a bit thin on the ground, but we can rely on wallflowers to provide a valuable source of early food.

Plant families

The majority of the flowers come from the Primary families; the others, and the framework plant, can be found in the Secondary families; only the tulips fall into the Other category.

Digitalis grandiflora (2 – see page 102)

Key to the Red and Yellow Border

Framework

Key reference	Plant	Units
A	*Rosa* 'Rose of Picardy'	x 1

Flowers

1	*Gaillardia* 'Oranges and Lemons'	x 3
2	*Digitalis grandiflora*	x 3
3	*Dahlia* 'Bishop of Llandaff'	x 3
4	*Rudbeckia hirta* 'Prairie Sun'	x 3
5	*Coreopsis* 'Limerock Passion'	x 3
6	*Achillea* 'Marmalade'	x 3
7	*Monarda didyma* 'Gardenview Scarlet'	x 3
8	*Doronicum* x *excelsum* 'Harpur Crewe'	x 3
9	*Verbascum* 'Gainsborough'	x 3
10	*Penstemon* 'Vanilla Plum'	x 3
11	*Helenium* 'Moerheim Beauty'	x 3

Fillers

F	A mixture to fill in gaps:	
	Erysimum cheiri – red variety	x 24
	Helianthus annuus 'Garden Statement'	x 12
	Papaver somniferum – red variety	x 12
X	*Tulipa*	x 45

(a mixture of yellow Single Early, Triumph, and Single Late to cover from early spring to very early summer)

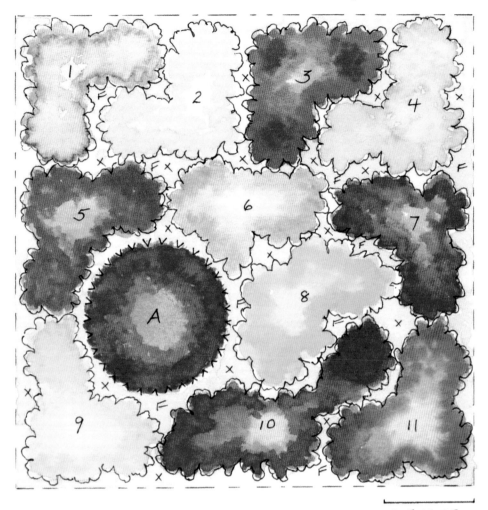

Plan for a Red and Yellow Border

Dahlia 'Bishop of Llandaff' (3)

Rudbeckia hirta 'Prairie Sun' (4)

Coreopsis 'Limerock Passion' (5)

Doronicum x *excelsum* 'Harpur Crewe' (8)

Penstemon 'Vanilla Plum' (10)

Helenium 'Moerheim Beauty' (11)

Flowering times of the
Red and Yellow Border

	Evergreen	Spring	Summer	Autumn
Erysimum cheiri	✓	✿		
Doronicum x *excelsum* 'Harpur Crewe'	✗	✿		
Tulipa	✗	✿		
Achillea 'Marmalade'	✗		✿	
Coreopsis 'Limerock Passion'	✗		✿	
Digitalis grandiflora	✓		✿	
Gaillardia 'Oranges and Lemons'	✗		✿	
Monarda didyma 'Gardenview Scarlet'	✗		✿	
Papaver somniferum	✗		✿	
Penstemon 'Vanilla Plum'	✗		✿	
Helenium 'Moerheim Beauty'	✗		✿	✿
Helianthus annuus 'Garden Statement'	✗		✿	✿
Rosa 'Rose of Picardy'	✗		✿	✿
Verbascum 'Gainsborough'	✗		✿	✿
Dahlia 'Bishop of Llandaff'	✗			✿
Rudbeckia hirta 'Prairie Sun'	✗			✿

Rainbow Border

This plan is for a bed 6 metres by 2 metres in size, backed by a fence; it could, of course, be extended or reduced depending on what space you have available. To extend it you may like to increase the number of plants in each of the colour sections; if you have to reduce the size, you may choose to leave out one colour section altogether.

I have more or less followed the approach often used in designing a 'colour' border: you start with cool colours like blues and purples at one end and finish with hot colours like orange and red at the other. I have altered the sequence a little, however, as we start with blue but end up with yellow, so we follow a slightly out-of-kilter rainbow, namely blue, indigo, violet, red, orange, yellow. Green is incorporated all through the border, of course, in the foliage.

You would be correct in thinking that it might be a little foolish to incorporate many red flowered plants in our design, since the majority of the red wavelength falls outside the visual spectrum of bees. The two flowers that we see as truly red, however, are attractive to bees for different reasons: the *Monarda* produces an abundance of nectar which the bees seem to be able to detect despite the colour of the flower; and although the *Dahlia* 'Bishop of Llandaff' has bright red marginal petals it has a ring of yellow florets which circle the centre of the flower, and this is what the bee sees.

Focus and framework

A focus doesn't feature in this plan but there are a number of framework plants, including two climbers – clematis and honeysuckle – which will clothe the fence at the back of the border. If you don't have a fence and want to treat this border as an 'island' bed, simply ignore the climbing plants altogether.

Flowers

Once again, flowers provide the main interest both in terms of colour and seasonality. I have arranged them in such a way that there is at least one specimen in flower in each of the seasons within the colour sections of the border. This will hopefully give an attractive display and also offer reasonable foraging for bees throughout the season.

Fillers

Tulipa and *Allium* fill the gaps in between the main planting. The *Tulipa* especially provide early season colour and a useful source of pollen for bees. The *Allium* are a tall, white variety with green centres to the individual flowers and, like other *Allium*, provide bees with a good deal of nectar during late spring and early summer.

Plant families

The Primary families of Asteraceae and Lamiaceae make up the bulk of the flowers. Secondary and Other families have an almost equal number of representatives, and these together add extra interest to the border in form and texture.

Caryopteris x *clandonensis* 'Worcester Gold' (C – see page 108)

Key to the Rainbow Border

Framework

Key reference	Plant	Units
C	*Caryopteris* x *clandonensis* 'Worcester Gold'	x 1
D	*Daphne tangutica*	x 1
E	*Clematis* 'Elsa Spath'	x 1
H	*Hypericum* 'Hidcote'	x 1
L	*Lonicera* x *tellmanniana*	x 1

Flowers

1	*Perovskia atriplicifolia* 'Little Spire'	x 3
2	*Aster* x *frikartii* 'Mönch'	x 3
3	*Lavandula angustifolia* 'Hidcote'	x 5
4	*Dahlia* 'Bishop of Llandaff'	x 3
5	*Achillea* 'Marmalade'	x 3
6	*Doronicum* x *excelsum* 'Harpur Crewe'	x 3
7	*Verbascum* 'Gainsborough'	x 3
8	*Anchusa azurea* 'Loddon Royalist'	x 3
9	*Ajuga reptens* 'Atropurpurea'	x 3
10	*Geranium* x *oxonianum* 'Claridge Druce'	x 3
11	*Echinacea purpurea*	x 3
12	*Monarda didyma* 'Gardenview Scarlet'	x 3
13	*Helenium* 'Waltraut'	x 3
14	*Kniphofia* 'Bees' Sunset'	x 3

Fillers

T	*Tulipa*	x 30
	(a mixture of white Single Early, Triumph, and Single Late to cover from early spring to very early summer)	
A	*Allium multibulbosum*	x 30

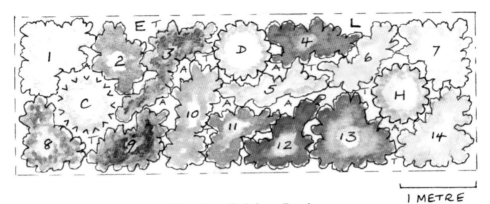

Plan for a Rainbow Border

Dahlia 'Bishop of Llandaff' (4)

Hypericum 'Hidcote' (H)

Achillea 'Marmalade' (5)

Verbascum 'Gainsborough' (7)

Geranium x *oxonianum* 'Claridge Druce' (10)

Monarda didyma 'Gardenview Scarlet' (12)

Helenium 'Waltraut' (13)

Lavandula angustifolia 'Hidcote' (3)

Anchusa azurea 'Loddon Royalist' (8)

Flowering times of the Rainbow Border

	Evergreen	Spring	Summer	Autumn
Ajuga reptens 'Atropurpurea'	✓	✿		
Allium multibulbosum	✗	✿		
Clematis 'Elsa Spath'	✗	✿		
Daphne tangutica	✓	✿		
Doronicum x *excelsum* 'Harpur Crewe'	✗	✿		
Tulipa	✗	✿		
Anchusa azurea 'Loddon Royalist'	✗	✿	✿	
Achillea 'Marmalade'	✗		✿	
Lavandula angustifolia 'Hidcote'	✓		✿	
Lonicera x *tellmanniana*	✗		✿	
Monarda didyma 'Gardenview Scarlet'	✗		✿	
Verbascum 'Gainsborough'	✗		✿	
Caryopteris x *clandonensis* 'Worcester Gold'	✗		✿	✿
Geranium x *oxonianum* 'Claridge Druce'	✗		✿	✿
Hypericum 'Hidcote'	✓		✿	✿
Kniphofia 'Bees' Sunset'	✗		✿	✿
Aster x *frikartii* 'Mönch'	✗			✿
Dahlia 'Bishop of Llandaff'	✗			✿
Echinacea purpurea	✗			✿
Helenium 'Waltraut'	✗			✿
Perovskia atriplicifolia 'Little Spire'	✗			✿

Garden Conditions

Within this design category you will find three plans for conditions in your garden which you have little control over: there is one for acid soil; one for alkaline soil; and one for a shady border.

Above: Erica x *darleyensis* 'Darley Dale' (B – see page 118)
Left: Calluna vulgaris 'Red Pimpernel' (C – see page 118)

Acid Soil Border

If your garden has predominantly acid soil then I should clean my spade straightaway and say that the number of bee-friendly plants that will grow in this type of soil is somewhat limited. The choice is narrow and for the most part is restricted to shrubby material. But within this limited range there are three species that stand out: *Erica, Calluna* and *Leptospermum.*

Heathers

The first two belong to the Ericaceae family and are commonly known by their collective name of heathers: *Erica* sp is more specifically called bell heather while *Calluna* sp is called ling. Together they provide a wide season of foraging for bees – in fact you can find one species or other of heather in flower throughout the year.

Commercial beekeepers will move their bees up to the heather moors where nothing else is in flower during late summer and early autumn in order to produce heather honey. They can guarantee that the heather is the only thing that the bees will have fed on, and therefore they can sell it as pure heather honey. (Bees will fly up to three miles for food but if they can find it on the hive-step they will not waste energy looking further afield.) This honey, often described as the 'Rolls Royce' of honey, is dark with an almost caramel flavour. You won't be able to produce this sort of monofloral honey from your own back garden, but if you do provide the bees with some heather they will thank you for it.

Manuka

Early summer onwards is when *Leptospermum scoparium* is in bloom. *Leptospermum,* otherwise known as tea tree or manuka, is for many people the ultimate bee shrub. (This is not the shrub that tea tree oil comes from, which is *Melaleuca alternifolia*; this is a good example of where knowing the Latin name prevents any confusion.) It is native to New Zealand where it can be found growing wild, but in England it is classed as half-hardy; it can just about cope with a couple of degrees below zero, but having neglected to protect mine one winter I lost it to nine degrees of frost. Despite the fact that it needs a little looking after in the winter months, it is well worth growing because bees love it.

The variety I have detailed for the planting plan is the straightforward single-flowered variety *Leptospermum scoparium*; you can get other varieties, like *L. scoparium* 'Apple Blossom' or *L. scoparium* 'Red Damask', but these have double flowers, so beware.

Other plants

The other plants I have suggested will all provide food for bees; one of them, *Vaccinium corymbosum*, will also provide us with a crop of fruit, since this is the bilberry (or blueberry, or whortleberry, depending on where you live).

You will notice that this plan is the exception to the rule as far as my 'Four Fs' (focus, framework, flowers and fillers), and 'planning according to plant families' tenet goes. For the most part the plants really fall into the framework definition with a few flowers thrown in. As for the families, it contains not one Primary family plant, and only one suggestion from the Secondary families. There is a simple reason for this: I could recall no plant from either Asteraceae or Lamiaceae that was both bee-friendly and acid-tolerant! I have instead relied heavily on the Ericaceae family, which, as their name implies, can cope with ericaceous conditions.

The planting plan covers an area of 5 metres by 4 metres, but can easily be adapted to suit a smaller or larger space.

Enkianthus campanulatus 'Pagoda Bush'
(E – see page 118)

Leptospermum scoparium
(S – see page 118)

Key to the Acid Soil Border

Key reference	Plant	Units
A	*Erica* x *darleyensis* 'White Glow'	x 7
B	*Erica* x *darleyensis* 'Darley Dale'	x 7
C	*Calluna vulgaris* 'Red Pimpernel'	x 7
D	*Calluna vulgaris* 'Silver Queen'	x 7
E	*Enkianthus campanulatus* 'Pagoda Bush'	x 3
G	*Gaultheria* x *wisleyensis* 'Wisley Pearl'	x 3
K	*Kalmia latifolia*	x 1
L	*Lithodora diffusa* 'Heavenly Blue'	x 12
S	*Leptospermum scoparium*	x 3
V	*Vaccinium corymbosum*	x 5

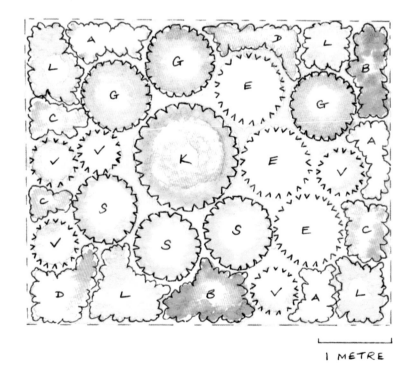

1 METRE

Plan for an Acid Soil Border

Flowering times of the Acid Soil Border

	Evergreen	Spring	Summer	Autumn
Enkianthus campanulatus 'Pagoda Bush'	✗	❁		
Erica x *darleyensis* 'Darley Dale'	✓	❁		
Erica x *darleyensis* 'White Glow'	✓	❁	❁	
Gaultheria x *wisleyensis* 'Wisley Pearl'	✓	❁	❁	
Leptospermum scoparium	✓	❁	❁	
Vaccinium corymbosum	✗	❁	❁	
Kalmia latifolia	✓		❁	
Lithodora diffusa 'Heavenly Blue'	✓		❁	
Calluna vulgaris 'Red Pimpernel'	✓		❁	❁
Calluna vulgaris 'Silver Queen'	✓		❁	❁

Artist's impression of an Acid Soil Border

Alkaline Soil Border

The range of plants that will grow in gardens with soil that veers towards the alkaline is far greater than those that will grow in acid soil. Indeed, a vast number of plants, although they do best in neutral soil, will tolerate alkaline conditions, while there are some plants that positively flourish if your conditions are a bit chalky. Having moved north, leaving Sussex and its downland soil behind, I sometimes yearn to be able to grow the magnificent specimens of *Campanula, Scabiosa, Sidalcea* and *Dianthus* which congregate in the garden memories of my childhood. I also recall some pretty sickly looking roses, so perhaps the garden wasn't quite as glorious as my memory would have it.

The plan is for an area of 6 metres by 2 metres, but it can be adapted to suit your needs. If the area is much smaller, I would recommend 'losing' one of the framework plants – probably the *Buddleja,* since the *Daphne* provides welcome food in spring for our buzzy friends. If your area is larger, then extend the planting by repeating a section of the plan.

Focus and framework

There is no focus plant in the plan, but the framework plants include a *Clematis,* which for me harks back to Sussex and its hedgerow-lined country lanes, full of the native *Clematis vitalba* or 'old man's beard', named after its whiskery seed heads which drape themselves like gossamer along the autumn hedgerow. The framework plants more or less follow on from one another in flowering season.

Flowers

Flowers make up the bulk of the planting. The plan I have devised includes the plants mentioned above, as well as others that will do well in alkaline soil, such as *Thalictrum* and *Erysimum.*

Fillers

Alliums form the fillers since they will cope with alkaline soil.

Plant families

I have chosen a good proportion of Primary family plants (mainly Asteraceae); some Secondary families and a good number of Other families offer a varied combination of form and texture.

Erysimum 'Winter Sorbet' (11– see page 122)

Key to the Alkaline Soil Border

Framework

Key reference	Plant	Units
B	*Buddleja davidii* 'Empire Blue'	x 1
C	*Clematis montana* 'Crinkle'	x 1
D	*Daphne tangutica*	x 1

Flowers

1	*Campanula lactiflora* 'Prichard's Variety'	x 3
2	*Thalictrum lucidum*	x 2
3	*Veronica longifolia* 'Romily Purple'	x 3
4	*Verbascum* 'Cherry Helen'	x 4
5	*Scabiosa caucasica* 'Clive Greaves'	x 3
6	*Echinops bannaticus* 'Blue Pearl'	x 3
7	*Papaver orientale* 'Patty's Plum'	x 4
8	*Achillea* 'Lilac Beauty'	x 3
9	*Echinacea purpurea* 'Sunrise'	x 3
10	*Helenium* 'Gartensonne'	x 3
11	*Erysimum* 'Winter Sorbet'	x 5
12	*Sidalcea* 'Sussex Beauty'	x 3
13	*Doronicum* x *excelsum* 'Harpur Crewe'	x 3
14	*Nepeta hybrida* 'Pink Candy'	x 3

Fillers

X	A mixture of:	x 45
	Allium 'Purple Sensation'	
	Allium sphaerocephalon	

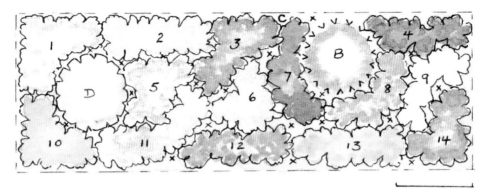

Plan for an Alkaline Soil Border

1 METRE

Campanula lactiflora 'Prichard's Variety' (1)

Buddleja davidii 'Empire Blue' (B)
Thalictrum lucidum (2)

Achillea 'Lilac Beauty' (8)
Echinacea purpurea 'Sunrise' (9)

Sidalcea 'Sussex Beauty' (12)
Nepeta hybrida 'Pink Candy' (14)

Flowering times of the Alkaline Soil Border

	Evergreen	Spring	Summer	Autumn
Daphne tangutica	✓	✻		
Doronicum x *excelsum* 'Harpur Crewe'	✗	✻		
Erysimum 'Winter Sorbet'	✓	✻		
Clematis montana 'Crinkle'	✗	✻	✻	
Achillea 'Lilac Beauty'	✗		✻	
Allium 'Purple Sensation'	✗		✻	
Allium sphaerocephalon	✗		✻	
Papaver orientale 'Patty's Plum'	✗		✻	
Scabiosa caucasica 'Clive Greaves'	✗		✻	
Sidalcea 'Sussex Beauty'	✗		✻	
Thalictrum lucidum	✗		✻	
Buddleja davidii 'Empire Blue'	✗		✻	✻
Campanula lactiflora 'Prichard's Variety'	✗		✻	✻
Echinops bannaticus 'Blue Pearl'	✗		✻	✻
Nepeta hybrida 'Pink Candy'	✗		✻	✻
Verbascum 'Cherry Helen'	✗		✻	✻
Veronica longifolia 'Romily Purple'	✗		✻	✻
Echinacea purpurea 'Sunrise'	✗			✻
Helenium 'Gartensonne'	✗			✻

Shade Border

We know that the majority of bee plants grow best in full sun, and bees often neglect flowers growing in the shade even though they are ones that we know are attractive to them. It must be said that there are very few bee-friendly plants that will grow successfully in *deep* shade – and even fewer bees that will visit them! But it may be that the only space you have to allocate to bee-friendly plants is in a shady area; even so, in compiling this border I have assumed that it gets some sun for at least part of the day.

The plan is for a fairly modest space, extending to 3 metres by 1 metre, but it can be adjusted to suit your particular area.

Focus and framework

In the plan as it stands there is little room for either a focus or any framework plants; however, if you have the opportunity to plant a larger area, you could include one or more *Skimmia* or *Mahonia*, both of which will cope with shady conditions.

Flowers

I have to come clean at this point and admit to my love of *Aconitum*. I know they are not bee plants *par excellence*, but I have always been fascinated by them. I'm not sure whether this is because of their common name of monkshood, or the more sinister wolfsbane, or the fact that, being toxic, they have to be treated with the utmost respect; but I have always felt that their tall spires of blue flowers add a certain presence to a shady border.

Many of the other flowers are ones that come more readily to mind when it comes to bee plants – *Geranium*, *Ajuga*, *Pulmonaria* and *Digitalis*, especially.

Fillers

In spring, gaps are filled with the delicate *Anemone nemerosa*. The ornamental dead nettle, *Lamium maculatum* 'Orchid Frost', can be relied upon from spring right through to autumn to provide extra forage for our buzzy friends, and during the times when it is not in flower, its foliage adds a silvery sheen to the ground cover.

Plant families

The majority of the plants fall into the Primary and Secondary families, with a smattering of Others, so even in a shady border we know that they are both bee-friendly and will give us a good mixture of form and texture.

Aconitum carmichaelii Wilsonii Group (3 – see page 130)

Astrantia major 'Venice' (2 – see page 130)

Aster divaricatus (4 – see page 130)

Heuchera 'Beaujolais' (7 – see page 130)

Ajuga reptens 'Atropurpurea' (9 – see page 130)

Key to the Shade Border

Flowers

Key reference	Plant	Units
1	*Doronicum* x *excelsum* 'Harpur Crewe', with	x 2
	Digitalis purpurea 'Pam's Choice'	x 2
2	*Astrantia major* 'Venice'	x 3
3	*Aconitum carmichaelii* Wilsonii Group	x 3
4	*Aster divaricatus*	x 2
5	*Geranium macrorrhizum* 'Mount Olympus White'	x 2
6	*Pulmonaria angustifolia* 'Mawson's Variety'	x 3
7	*Heuchera* 'Beaujolais'	x 2
8	*Geranium macrorrhizum* 'Ingwersen's Variety'	x 3
9	*Ajuga reptens* 'Atropurpurea'	x 3

Fillers

L	*Lamium maculatum* 'Orchid Frost'	x 4
X	*Anemone nemerosa* 'Alba'	x 12
	Anemone nemerosa 'Allenii'	x 12
	Anemone nemerosa 'Pentre Pink'	x 12

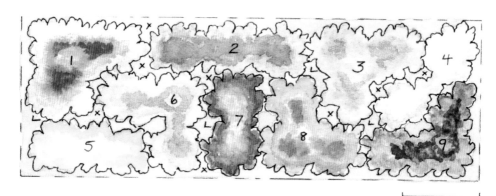

0.5 METRE

Plan for a Shade Border

Flowering times of the Shade Border

	Evergreen	Spring	Summer	Autumn
Ajuga reptens 'Atropurpurea'	✓	✽		
Anemone nemerosa 'Alba'	✗	✽		
Anemone nemerosa 'Allenii'	✗	✽		
Anemone nemerosa 'Pentre Pink'	✗	✽		
Doronicum x *excelsum* 'Harpur Crewe'	✗	✽		
Pulmonaria angustifolia 'Mawson's Variety'	✗	✽		
Geranium macrorrhizum 'Ingwersen's Variety'	✓	✽	✽	
Geranium macrorrhizum 'Mount Olympus White'	✓	✽	✽	
Lamium maculatum 'Orchid Frost'	✓	✽	✽	✽
Astrantia major 'Venice'	✗		✽	
Digitalis purpurea 'Pam's Choice'	✗		✽	
Heuchera 'Beaujolais'	✓		✽	
Aconitum carmichaelii Wilsonii Group	✗			✽
Aster divaricatus	✗			✽

Utility Gardens

I have called this group of plans 'utility' because they include ideas for practical as well as decorative use of the spaces. Here you will find plans for a cutting garden, a herb garden, and a garden filled with flowers, fruit and vegetables.

Above: Agastache 'Black Adder' (2 – see page 136)
Left: Verbena bonariensis (10 – see page 136)

Cutting Spiral

I love to have flowers in the house, especially ones that I have cut from the garden. My garden isn't big enough to have a separate cutting patch, but if it were I would like to have something different from the usual regimented straight lines which, although allowing easy access and cultivation, remind me too much of my granddad's rows of dahlias, which produced a better harvest of earwigs than blooms most years.

No, I would like something more whimsical, so I have designed a 'snail shell' plot, based on the Fibonacci spiral (and I would put up a sign to the effect that this would be the only snail allowed in my garden!). The flowers are still easy to get to via a main path, and smaller paths between the blocks of flowers, so cultivation and maintenance would not pose a problem. I should say that the flowers included here are my favourites, and I know that bees like them too, but you could easily make substitutions.

Because these are flowers for cutting, I have abandoned the usual blueprint of focus, framework, flowers and filler plants; they are all decorative, otherwise they wouldn't look good in a vase! Instead, I have split them into sections of perennials and annuals, with some tulips edging the main path. Although not strictly speaking an annual, I have included *Dahlia* in this section since, being tender, its tubers need to be lifted and stored each autumn.

A major point to remember when you are growing flowers both for cutting and for bees is that the optimum time for the 'harvest' of each is different. If you want the maximum vase-life from your flowers you must cut them before you see any loose pollen. This is because the flower is a plant's reproduction mechanism. It is there to attract pollinating insects; once pollinated, the seed will grow and the flower itself will die away. Most species can be cut in the bud stage, as long as there is some petal colour showing, or when the petals have just begun to unfurl. (Dahlias are the exception – only cut these when they are fully open, but before the pollen starts to loosen.) But we want to provide food for bees, too, so it follows that we must allow some of the flowers to release pollen.

The best way forward, I think, is that for every stem you cut, leave one for the bees – that way everybody's happy!

Penstemon 'Tubular Bells Pink' (7 – see page 136)

Key to the Cutting Spiral

Perennials

Key reference	Plant	Units
1	*Achillea* 'Apfelblüte'	x 4
2	*Agastache* 'Black Adder'	x 4
3	*Allium sphaerocephalon*	x 50
4	*Campanula glomerata*	x 4
5	*Astrantia major* 'Moulin Rouge'	x 4
6	*Echinops ritro* 'Veitch's Blue'	x 4
7	*Penstemon* 'Tubular Bells Pink'	x 4
8	*Eryngium* x *tripartitum* 'Jade Frost'	x 4
9	*Aster* x *frikartii* 'Mönch'	x 4
10	*Verbena bonariensis*	x 9
11	*Veronica longifolia* 'Romily Purple'	x 4
12	*Scabiosa caucasica* 'Clive Greaves'	x 4
13	*Echinacea purpurea*	x 4
14	*Helenium* 'Gartensonne'	x 4

Annuals

15	*Ammi majus*	1 packet
16	*Callistephus chinensis* (single flowered varieties)	1 packet
17	*Nigella damascena*	1 packet
18	*Dahlia* 'Bishop of York'	x 6

Bulbs

X	*Tulipa* (various)	x 60

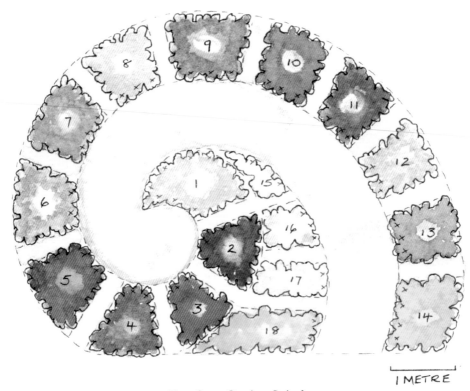

Plan for a Cutting Spiral

Allium sphaerocephalon (3)

Astrantia major 'Moulin Rouge' (5)

Eryngium x *tripartitum* 'Jade Frost' (8)

Aster x *frikartii* 'Mönch' (9)

Scabiosa caucasica 'Clive Greaves' (12)

Echinacea purpurea (13)

Helenium 'Gartensonne' (14)

Flowering times of the Cutting Spiral

	Evergreen	Spring	Summer	Autumn
Tulipa	✗	❁		
Allium sphaerocephalon	✗		❁	
Ammi majus	✗		❁	
Astrantia major 'Moulin Rouge'	✗		❁	
Callistephus chinensis	✗		❁	
Campanula glomerata	✗		❁	
Echinops ritro 'Veitch's Blue'	✗		❁	
Eryngium x *tripartitum* 'Jade Frost'	✗		❁	
Nigella damascena	✗		❁	
Penstemon 'Tubular Bells Pink'	✗		❁	
Scabiosa caucasica 'Clive Greaves'	✗		❁	
Verbena bonariensis	✗		❁	
Achillea 'Apfelblüte'	✗		❁	❁
Agastache 'Black Adder'	✗		❁	❁
Veronica longifolia 'Romily Purple'	✗		❁	❁
Aster x *frikartii* 'Mönch'	✗			❁
Dahlia 'Bishop of York'	✗			❁
Echinacea purpurea	✗			❁
Helenium 'Gartensonne'	✗			❁

Herb Garden

When it comes to herbs I am usually drawn towards culinary ones. I use no end of them in cooking, from the robust winter savory (*Satureja montana*) in hearty casseroles to the delicate chive flowers in a summer salad. And where would stuffing be without sage! And they are excellent bee plants, of course. So, inevitably, here is a plan for culinary herbs.

As I was doodling around with shapes for a design I found myself coming back to a hexagon – yes, I know it's a little clichéd when it comes to bees, but it does have a pleasing symmetry to it. I then found myself dividing it into three; one thing led to another and I ended up with a herb garden that covers three different uses: herbs for cooking, herbs for fragrance, and herbs for cosmetics. (I have deliberately steered clear of medicinal herbs, which require specialist knowledge and are not to be dabbled with indiscriminately.)

The entire plan covers an area of roughly 5.5 metres by 6 metres. Although I have divided it into three separate sections, you could, for example, leave out the 'cosmetic' planting and double up on culinary herbs instead, or have a garden entirely given over to fragrant herbs – the choice is yours, and the plan is there to be altered and adapted.

Focus and framework

At the centre of the design is the apothecary's rose (*Rosa gallica* var. *officinalis*), which is not only special in its own right, but it can be used for all three purposes: its petals can be used fresh in desserts; its fragrance is almost unsurpassed; and everyone has heard of rosewater, traditionally made using the flowers of the apothecary's rose.

Enclosing the beds is *Teucrium* x *lucidrys*, commonly known as wall germander. Prior to the 17th century, this plant was used extensively in knot gardens; later, box took over as the favoured edging plant. We may find that it comes back into fashion as the dreaded blight disease takes its toll on our box hedges. Indeed, during a visit to the magnificent gardens at Highgrove, the residence of HRH The Prince of Wales and the Duchess of Cornwall, I noticed that much of the box edging in the walled garden has been replaced by wall germander. Although compared to box it is lax in its habit, the beautiful pink flowers of the germander attract no end of bees and other insects, so to my mind it is allowed to be a little wayward! After flowering it can easily be trimmed back into shape.

Flowers

You will see that three of the herbs (rosemary, lavender and thyme), have found their way into each of the beds, which goes to show just how versatile they are.

Bed A – Culinary herbs

This bed contains the obvious candidates that most cooks wouldn't be without – sage, thyme, chives, and so on. The obvious omission is mint; although a brilliant bee plant if left to flower, it is rampant in its desire to explore beyond the confines of its allotted space – as every gardener who has planted one knows. You could replace the winter savory with mint grown in a pot and then sunk into the ground, but I think winter savory is an underrated and underused herb so I have given it space in this garden.

You may be surprised to see lavender in a culinary herb bed, but its flowers can be used in both savoury and sweet recipes, and I particularly like scones with lavender flowers, especially if they are topped with home-made lemon curd.

Bed B – Fragrant herbs

This is my potpourri patch – all the herbs (and the rose, of course) have either fragrant flowers or leaves. They make superb ingredients for a home-grown potpourri, and all except one produce flowers that are good for bees. The exception is *Iris germanica* 'Florentina', which I have included because the dried root is traditionally used as a fragrance fixative in potpourri. And although the *Viola tricolor* doesn't figure highly in the best plants for bees chart, the almost cheeky expression on the face of its flower is a lovely addition to our fragrant mix.

Bed C – Cosmetic herbs

Although I would never encourage anyone to self-medicate, many herbs, some of which I have included here, can be safely used in topical cosmetics, such as hand creams and bath preparations. For example, the flowers of *Chamaemelum nobile* (chamomile) or *Calendula officinalis* (pot marigold) can be added to base cream to use on the hands; an infusion of rosemary, lavender or sage leaves can be used as a hair rinse. Traditionally the leaves and roots of *Saponaria officinalis* were used to produce a cleansing lather – its common name, soapwort, is a giveaway! And when crushed, the seeds of *Daucus carota* (wild carrot), which are high in vitamin A, can be used in skin cream. (It is easy to confuse wild carrot with other species; the characteristic that sets it apart is the tiny maroon-red flower right at the centre of the inflorescence. Tie a piece of string around the stem to identify it, to make it easy to collect seeds in the autumn.)

Experiment with a few herbs, even if it is just a sprig of lavender in the bath – an excuse to lie back and relax.

Plant families

As you might expect, Primary families, especially Lamiaceae, are the mainstay of the herb garden, with just one from a Secondary family, Rosaceae, and the rest coming from Other families. Nevertheless, there is a good mixture of plants for both us and the bees.

Daucus carota (C8 – see page 144)

Rosa gallica var. *officinalis* (R – see page 144)

Key to the Herb Garden

Focus and framework

Key reference	Plant	Units
R	*Rosa gallica* var. *officinalis*	x 1
	Teucrium x *lucidrys*, clipped (hedging)	x 210

Flowers

Bed A – Culinary herbs

1	*Rosmarinus officinalis*, standard	x 1
2	*Lavandula angustifolia* 'Hidcote'	x 6
3	*Thymus* 'Jekka'	x 12
4	*Allium schoenoprasum* (chives)	x 50
5	*Satureja montana* (winter savory)	x 5
6	*Salvia officinalis* Purpurascens Group (sage)	x 5
7	*Origanum vulgare*	x 5
8	*Petroselinum crispum* (parsley)	x 5

Bed B – Fragrant herbs

1	*Rosmarinus officinalis*, standard	x 1
2	*Lavandula angustifolia* 'Hidcote'	x 6
3	*Thymus citriodorus* 'Silver Queen'	x 12
4	*Nepeta hybrida* 'Pink Candy'	x 40
5	*Reseda odorata*	x 5
6	*Aloysia triphylla*	x 5
7	*Iris germanica* 'Florentina'	x 4
8	*Viola tricolor*	x 9

Bed C – Cosmetic herbs

1	*Rosmarinus officinalis*, standard	x 1
2	*Lavandula angustifolia* 'Hidcote'	x 6
3	*Thymus vulgaris*	x 12
4	*Chamaemelum nobile*	x 40
5	*Calendula officinalis*	x 5
6	*Saponaria officinalis*	x 5
7	*Origanum vulgare*	x 5
8	*Daucus carota*	x 5

BED A

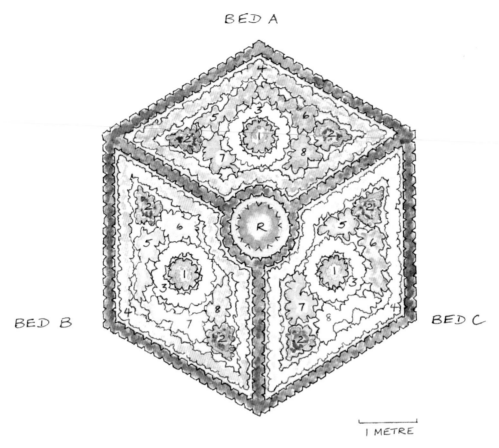

BED B

BED C

1 METRE

Plan for a Herb Garden

Teucrium x *lucidrys*

Teucrium x *lucidrys* and *Buxus sempervirens 'Suffruticosa'*

Allium schoenoprasum and *Salvia officinalis* Purpurascens Group (A4, A6)

Rosmarinus officinalis and *Thymus vulgaris* (C1, C3)

Viola tricolour (B8)

Calendula officinalis (C5)

Flowering times of the Herb Garden

	Evergreen	Spring	Summer	Autumn
Rosmarinus officinalis	✓	❀		
Iris germanica 'Florentina'	✓	❀	❀	
Viola tricolor	✗	❀	❀	❀
Aloysia triphylla	✗		❀	
Calendula officinalis	✗		❀	
Chamaemelum nobile	✗		❀	
Daucus carota	✗		❀	
Lavandula angustifolia 'Hidcote'	✓		❀	
Origanum vulgare	✓		❀	
Petroselinum crispum	✓		❀	
Reseda odorata	✗		❀	
Rosa gallica var. *officinalis*	✗		❀	
Salvia officinalis Purpurascens Group	✓		❀	
Saponaria officinalis	✗		❀	
Satureja montana	✓		❀	
Teucrium x *lucidrys*	✓		❀	
Thymus 'Jekka'	✓		❀	
Thymus citriodorus 'Silver Queen'	✓		❀	
Thymus vulgaris	✓		❀	
Allium schoenoprasum	✗		❀	❀
Nepeta hybrida 'Pink Candy'	✗		❀	❀

Flower, Fruit and Vegetable Border

I included plans for a large and small potager in my previous book *The Bee Garden*, but I couldn't miss the opportunity to include another one here. Having said that, when I think of the term 'potager' it conjures up a vision of a posh vegetable garden with some flowers added, whereas in this plan the emphasis is equally on flowers and herbs as on vegetables. In fact, the range of vegetables is limited and I have chosen them as much for their decorative quality as for their utility. You can, of course, change or adapt these plans to suit your own situation, so if you want to replace some of the flowers with vegetables, or not bother with some of the herbs, then that's fine – it's your garden!

Not everyone has space for a dedicated vegetable patch, which is one reason why I came up with the idea of incorporating a good number of flowers and herbs. I also thought that a 'modular' system based on an area measuring 2 metres by 2 metres would be a novel way of making the idea accessible to nearly everyone, from those of us with a modest back garden to others who have a much larger space to fill. Each module could be divided in four sections (A to D), so that a rotation system for vegetables could be maintained – more on that below.

The plan as it stands is for an area of 2 metres by 4 metres, covering a space equivalent to two modules, so that each of the groups of planting signified by a letter, A to D, occupies half a 'module' area. If you have enough space for four modules, you can allocate a whole module to each of the letters, and so on.

Focus and framework

With regard to information on which apples to choose, have a look at the information given in the plan for a Large Cottage Garden Border (see page 49).

For this plan I have chosen four varieties: 'Egremont Russet' and 'Red Windsor', both in pollination group B, and 'James Grieve' and 'Sunset', which are in pollination group C. These should be trained as 'step over apples'; they are trees on a dwarfing rootstock that have a very short centre stem of about 30cm – low enough to step over, hence the name – with a horizontal branch either side. They are both attractive and productive.

In the centre of the whole design is the pink rose 'Scintillation', whose lax habit makes it ideal for tying to a wigwam; it is not as vigorous as a climber or rambler but will reach 2 metres. It has lovely red hips in the autumn and is fragrant to boot, so just right for us and the bees.

Each of the modules has, as its focus, a wigwam made from hazel poles, up which runner beans and squash are grown. The flowers of the runner beans are beautiful in their own right; indeed, these plants were grown for their flowers long before it dawned on anyone to eat the beans! Although we are used to seeing squash growing on the ground (think of pumpkins), many varieties can easily be grown vertically, as long as the support is stout enough to tie the fruits to if necessary.

Flowers, herbs and vegetables

In this plan we find herbs and vegetables as well as flowers. I would like to talk a bit about the vegetables, as they are unique to this plan of the selection in this book.

The groups of vegetables are ordered in such a way that it should be fairly easy to keep to a rotational planting regime, whereby the same type of vegetable is not grown in the same place each year – in fact, it should be five years before your peas are back to where they started. In the first year you would plant up according to the plan; the next year, you shift things round in a clockwise direction so that Bed A is planted up with what was in Bed B the previous year, and so on.

So in Year 1, Bed A has *Alliums* (garlic, leeks); Bed B has legumes (broad beans, peas); Bed C has brassicas (sprouting broccoli, cavolo nero); and Bed D has roots (carrots, parsnips). In Year 2, Bed A has the legumes, Bed B has brassicas, Bed C has roots, and Bed D has *Alliums*. And so on.

The main reason for rotating crops is to prevent a build-up of diseases and pests that target particular types of plants. If you don't grow the same thing in the same place year on year then the disease has less chance to get a foothold. Another reason is that some vegetables require more nutrients than others. The legume family 'fix' nitrogen in the soil, a nutrient for which the brassica family is hungry, so it makes sense to follow peas and beans with kale or broccoli.

I have indicated precise vegetables in the key – these are the ones that I would grow because I like them and they fit in with the rotation. If you don't want to grow garlic, this could be replaced by onions – still a member of the *Allium* family – and if you can't stand parsnips, then how about some celeriac?

If you wish to keep seed from your favourite vegetables then you must obviously allow some of them to flower – even the broccoli and carrots! This is where the bees come in, of course. A note of caution here if you do want to collect seed for next year's crop: make sure that you grow 'traditional' varieties, not F1 hybrids, which will not come true from seed. Varieties marked 'heirloom' can be worth growing because they are often closer to the original species than modern hybrids.

Some vegetables can be slotted in anywhere there is space because they hold no threat of disease to other vegetables. These include leafy salad crops such as lettuce and rocket, also spinach and chard.

Obviously all the flowering fruit and vegetables will be a magnet for bees, and the harvest will increase as a result: it has been estimated that fruit and vegetable yields can be increased by anything up to 36 per cent if bees are active on the crop, so it's a real win-win situation.

In contrast to the vegetables, which are shifted round each year, the flowers and herbs are permanent. I have chosen the flowers so that there is something in bloom throughout the 'bee season', plus a number of them are good for cutting; and if you let some of the herbs flower the bees will be ecstatic!

Fillers

As well as tulips to carry the plot through spring into summer, when the lovely compact maroon *Allium sphaerocephalon* takes up the baton, I have suggested planting alpine strawberries (*Fragaria vesca*) between the stepping stones.

Plant families

Primary families Asteraceae and Lamiaceae feature strongly in the herbs and flowering plants; unsurprisingly, neither is to be found among the vegetables. The Secondary family Rosaceae features in the focus and framework; Other families account for the vegetables.

Key to the Flower, Fruit and Vegetable Border

Focus and framework

Key reference	Plant	Units
R	*Rosa* 'Scintillation', grown up a wigwam	x 1
M	*Malus domestica* (apple), grown as 'step over' trees:	
	Egremont Russet (Group B)	x 1
	Red Windsor (Group B)	x 1
	James Grieve (Group C)	x 1
	Sunset (Group C)	x 1
W	Runner beans and Squash, trained up hazel poles	

Flowers

Bed A

1	*Thymus vulgaris* 'Compactus'	x 3
2	Leeks	
3	*Doronicum* 'Miss Mason'	x 2
4	*Calendula officinalis*	x 3
5	Garlic	
6	*Achillea* 'Pretty Belinda'	x 1

Bed B

1	*Hyssopus officinalis*	x 2
2	Peas	
3	*Aster* x *frikartii* 'Mönch'	x 1
4	*Allium schoenoprasum*	x 5
5	Broad beans	
6	*Nepeta racemosa* 'Walker's Low'	x 2

Bed C

1	*Origanum vulgare*	x 3
2	Cavolo nero (Tuscan kale)	
3	*Pulmonaria* 'Cotton Cool'	x 1

4	*Rosmarinus officinalis*	x 1
5	Sprouting broccoli	
6	*Echinops bannaticus* 'Blue Pearl'	x 1

Bed D

1	*Salvia officinalis*	x 3
2	Carrots	
3	*Lavandula angustifolia* 'Hidcote'	x 2
4	*Satureja montana*	x 5
5	Parsnips	
6	*Helenium* 'Kanaria'	x 2

Fillers

| X | A mixture of spring and summer flowering bulbs: | x 50 |

Tulipa (a mixture of Single Early, Triumph, and Single Late to cover from early spring to very early summer)

Allium sphaerocephalon

| F | *Fragaria vesca* | x 16 |

(planted between stepping stones)

Leafy vegetables and salad crops to fill in anywhere, such as: Lettuce, Rocket, Spinach, Swiss Chard

0·5 METRE

Plan for a Flower, Fruit and Vegetable Border

Thymus vulgaris 'Compactus' (A1)

Leeks (A2)

Achillea 'Pretty Belinda' (A6)

Aster x *frikartii* 'Mönch' (B3)

Cavolo nero (C2)

Echinops bannaticus 'Blue Pearl' (C6)

Runner beans (W)

Peas with Lettuce (B2)

Satureja montana (D4)

Helenium 'Kanaria' (D6)

Allium sphaerocephalon (X)

Fragaria vesca (F)

Sprouting broccoli, left to flower (C5)

Flowering times of the
Flower, Fruit and Vegetable Border

	Evergreen	Spring	Summer	Autumn
Doronicum 'Miss Mason'	✗	✤		
Malus domestica	✗	✤		
Pulmonaria 'Cotton Cool'	✗	✤		
Rosmarinus officinalis	✓	✤		
Tulipa	✗	✤		
Allium schoenoprasum	✗		✤	
Allium sphaerocephalon	✗		✤	
Broad beans	✗		✤	
Calendula officinalis	✗		✤	
Echinops bannaticus 'Blue Pearl'	✗		✤	
Fragaria vesca	✓		✤	
Hyssopus officinalis	✓		✤	
Lavandula angustifolia 'Hidcote'	✓		✤	
Nepeta racemosa 'Walker's Low'	✗		✤	
Origanum vulgare	✓		✤	
Runner beans	✗		✤	
Salvia officinalis	✓		✤	
Satureja montana	✓		✤	
Squash	✗		✤	
Thymus vulgaris 'Compactus'	✓		✤	
Achillea 'Pretty Belinda'	✗		✤	✤
Helenium 'Kanaria'	✗		✤	✤
Rosa 'Scintillation'	✗		✤	✤
Aster x *frikartii* 'Mönch'	✗			✤

A Beekeeper's Garden

This plan came about quite serendipitously. I was approached by a beekeeping friend of mine to redesign his back garden. He was tired, he said, of looking out on to a mangy rectangle of lawn with a few scraggy plants making a desperate attempt to grow in the borders surrounding it. (His words, not mine, but I have to agree with him!) And, being a beekeeper, he thought it was about time he put into practice what he was constantly advising others to do, and that was to provide a decent location for bees to flourish.

As well as being a good place to keep his bees, he wanted his garden to be attractive for him and his wife. His specifications included having a paved area near the house big enough for a table and chairs, a lawn, space for a shed and a greenhouse, and somewhere to grow some vegetables.

His request came at just about the same time as I was just putting finishing touches to some of the planting plans for this book. The solution was obvious: why not use some of the plans I had already created and bring them together in one garden? And so the Beekeeper's Garden was born.

You will see from the key that I have included five of the plans (and one of them twice). They will all have to be adapted slightly to fit the spaces allocated to them, but the overall essence of each of the designs can be preserved.

Bed 1, near to the beehives (B), comprises an extended version of the Native Naturalistic Border. This seemed to me an appropriate type of planting to have in proximity to the hives.

Nearby is a water trough (T), which will provide a source of water close enough to the hives for the bees to find it, but not so close that they will be disturbed when it is topped up.

I have added a tree (2) to the garden in the shape of a crab apple, *Malus* 'John Downie', which will have a beautiful display of blossom in the spring and provide a pollination partner for the other apple trees in the garden.

Other apple trees can be found in Bed 3, the Large Cottage Garden Border. They are trained as espaliers against a post and wire 'trellis' at the back of the border (D), which also loosely divides the 'bee' area from the 'leisure' part of the garden.

Standing in the border, and in line with the centre of the patio doors to make a focal point when viewed from the house, there will be a sculpture, or artwork. My friend hasn't quite decided what form this will take; it may even be a sundial. (I have suggested a life-size model of him in his bee suit but his wife was not impressed!)

In the 'leisure' part of the garden, either side of the lawn and the paved area, are two Large Traditional Borders (4 and 5), which are tweaked a little in order to be accommodated in the space.

To add height to the whole garden, and to divide the 'leisure' and 'utility' areas, I have incorporated a pergola, up which climbers such as *Clematis* or *Rosa* can be trained.

As well as a shed and greenhouse in the 'utility' area, I have included a cold frame, lean-to (somewhere dry to keep the wheelbarrow, pots, and so on), compost bins and a comfrey (*Symphytum*) patch (for making comfrey fertilizer).

There is a separate area (7) for growing bush fruit (gooseberries and currants, both black and red) and cane fruit (raspberries and blackberries). This is next to the vegetable garden (8): the original plan, which included a number of flowers, will be altered so that they (the flowers) will be replaced by vegetables. The beekeeper is keen on growing some shallots and onions and these will be incorporated into Bed A. In Bed B there will be some more peas and French beans. Bed C will have some cabbages and Brussels sprouts added to the kale and broccoli, and in Bed D there will be more carrots and some celeriac.

Bed 9, which faces north, is where an extended Shade Border will be planted; next to it, in Bed 10, the Cultivated Naturalistic Border will find a home.

Hedges (H), partly made up of hawthorn (*Crataegus monogyna*), sloe (*Prunus spinosa*), dog rose (*Rosa canina*), and honeysuckle (*Lonicera periclymenum*), already surround the garden on three sides; they make an ideal boundary for bees, not only in terms of providing food, but also giving shelter from the prevailing south-westerly winds.

As far as the hard landscaping goes, the patio area and some of the paths will be made by re-laying the York stone slabs that are already in the garden. The other paths will be made from self-binding gravel edged with setts. The self-binding gravel is hard-wearing, relatively inexpensive and will sit well in the rural location.

All in all, I think the bees will be happy with the overall design – and I hope my friend will be too!

Key to the Beekeeper's Garden

Key reference

A	Artwork or sculpture
B	Beehive
C	Compost bins
D	Dividing trellis
F	Cold frame
G	Greenhouse
H	Existing hedge
L	Lean-to
P	Pergola
S	Shed
T	Water trough
W	Existing wall
1	Extended Native Naturalistic Border
2	*Malus* 'John Downie'
3	Large Cottage Border
4	Adapted Large Traditional Border
5	Adapted Large Traditional Border
6	Comfrey patch
7	Bush and cane fruit
8	Flowers, fruit and vegetable area
9	Extended Shade Border
10	Cultivated Naturalistic Border

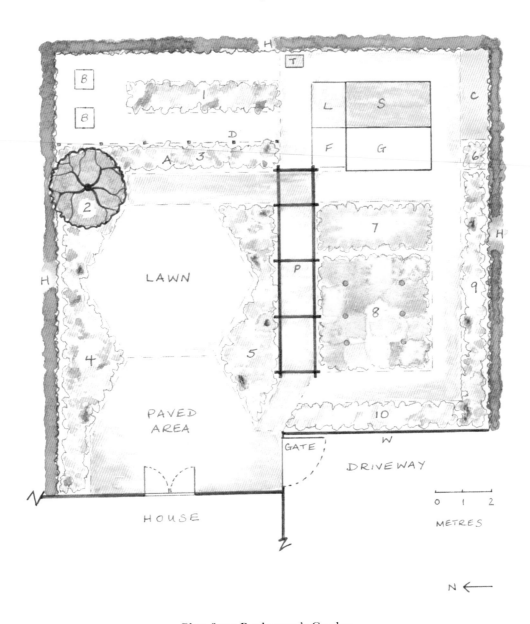

Plan for a Beekeeper's Garden

Container Planting

Even if you don't have a garden, you can grow bee-friendly plants by using containers and pots. And if you do have a garden you can still plant up some containers to fill in gaps or frame a doorway.

Growing plants in containers means that you have control over the growing medium, so you can grow whatever you choose. The other main advantage is that they are portable – unless they are so big and heavy that it would take an Olympic weightlifter to move them! From a design point of view, they create an instant focal point – very useful as an interim measure.

There are some disadvantages of growing in containers. The first is that the plants will soon use the available nutrients in the compost, and because their roots are restricted they cannot search down into the soil for food. You will have to provide food for them in the shape of some sort of fertilizer. The second disadvantage is watering. Moisture will evaporate far quicker from a container than from open soil, which means that during the summer months your pots will undoubtedly need to be watered every day and sometimes twice a day. As a rough guide, 2.5 cm (1 inch) of water will penetrate about 15–20cm (6–8 inches) of soil, so you can see that even if it rains you will still have to top up your containers.

But don't let this put you off growing some bee-friendly plants in containers. Given even a modicum of care you can supply a modest amount of food for bees throughout the growing season.

The type of container you use will depend very much on personal choice. I love terracotta pots: their colour, texture, different sizes and shapes, and the way they 'weather'. Whatever I plant in them 'looks' right. But there are no end of other pots and containers available, from purpose-made to 'make do'. A friend of mine gets hold of old wine boxes from her local vintner, drills holes in the bottom, and plants them up with herbs and annuals and uses them as window boxes. Yes, the wood deteriorates after a time but they last long enough for her purposes.

And why not plant up some bee-friendly hanging baskets?

What to grow? Just about any plant will survive in a container, with a little care, so as long as it's bee-friendly, grow whatever takes your fancy. There are very few bee-friendly plants that will flower all year round; gorse

(*Ulex europaeus*) is one of them but I'm not sure I would want a pot of gorse taking pride of place in my garden! The answer is perhaps to have a succession of pots, one (or more) for each season, so that as one fades it is replaced by the next.

Here are a few ideas to give you some inspiration.

Muscari armeniacum

Plants for Spring Containers

• Try *Rosmarinus officinalis*, *Lamium maculatum* 'Orchid Frost' and *Muscari armeniacum*.

• A small *Skimmia* x *confusa* 'Kew Green' can be planted with *Erysimum cheiri* 'Primrose Bedder' and *Ajuga reptens* 'Atropurpurea'. Include some *Crocus*, too – perhaps some yellow or purple-flowered ones to tone in with the other plants.

• An alternative is to have a pot full of spring flowering bulbs – they will vary on the bee-friendly chart, but *Crocus* and *Muscari* especially will be attractive to bees at this time.

A selection of plants for Spring Containers

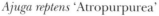
Ajuga reptens 'Atropurpurea'   *Crocus*

Rosmarinus officinalis

Lamium maculatum 'Orchid Frost'

Skimmia x *confusa* 'Kew Green'

Erysimum cheiri 'Primrose Bedder'

Plants for Summer Containers

Where to begin? There are endless permutations of flowers for our buzzy friends during this season – here are just a few.

- *Achillea* 'Pretty Belinda' will look attractive with *Lavandula angustifolia* 'Hidcote', *Penstemon* 'Blackberry Fudge' and *Heliotropium arborescens*.
- And how about *Liatris spicata* with *Geranium* 'Patricia', *Allium sphaerocephalon* and *Iberis umbellata*?
- Or try *Monarda* 'Aquarius' with *Cosmos bipinnatus*, *Echium* 'Blue Bedder' and *Hyssopus officinalis*.
- *Echinops bannaticus* 'Blue Pearl', *Verbascum* 'Sierra Sunset', *Nigella damascena* and *Calendula officinalis* would make a good combination.

A selection of plants for Summer Containers

Achillea 'Pretty Belinda'   *Lavandula angustifolia* 'Hidcote'

Penstemon 'Blackberry Fudge'

Liatris spicata

Echium 'Blue Bedder'

Hyssopus officinalis

Heliotropium arborescens

Allium sphaerocephalon

Geranium 'Patricia'

Iberis umbellata

Monarda 'Aquarius'

Cosmos bipinnatus

Plants for Autumn Containers

There are lots of plants that will do well, and look good together, in pots in the autumn.

- How about *Aconitum carmichaelii* Wilsonii Group 'Spaetlese', *Aster novi-belgii* 'Dandy' with *Echinacea purpurea* 'Pow Wow' and *Heuchera* 'Bressingham Bronze'?
- *Kniphofia* 'Bressingham Comet', *Dahlia* 'Moonfire', *Viola tricolor* and *Salvia officinalis* Purpurascens Group will complement one another well.
- Or try *Rudbeckia hirta* 'Prairie Sun' with *Dahlia* 'Romeo' and *Verbascum* 'Gainsborough'.

A selection of plants for Autumn Containers

Kniphofia 'Bressingham Comet'   *Aconitum carmichaelii* Wilsonii Group 'Spaetlese'

Aster novi-belgii 'Dandy'

Echinacea purpurea 'Pow Wow'

Heuchera 'Bressingham Bronze'

Dahlia 'Moonfire'

Viola tricolor

Salvia officinalis Purpurascens Group

Herbs in Containers

A huge number of herbs are excellent bee plants if you let them flower, and are also superb container plants. Almost any combination of the herbs featured in the Herb Garden plan (see page 140) would provide a first-rate display.

Culinary herbs

A container planted up with some culinary herbs would be ideal to stand outside the kitchen door, provided it isn't in too much shade. The combinations of culinary herbs are endless, but here are a couple

- How about a 'Scarborough Fair' pot? *Petroselinum crispum, Salvia officinalis, Rosmarinus officinalis* and *Thymus vulgaris* – in other words, parsley, sage, rosemary and thyme! All are useful in no end of recipes.
- Or perhaps try a container of winter herbs which you could allow to flower in the summer and then dead-head so that the foliage is available during the winter. This would work with herbs such as *Thymus vulgaris* (thyme), *Hyssopus officinalis* (hyssop), *Satureja montana* (winter savory), and the hardy oregano, *Origanum vulgare*.
- Last summer I planted a 'Pimms and Pasta' pot which was a great hit with the bees – and it made a brilliant talking point during a barbecue with friends. I planted up *Borago officinalis* (borage) and *Mentha spicata* var. *crispa* 'Moroccan' (Moroccan mint) for the Pimms, with *Ocimum basilicum* (basil) and *Origanum majorana* (sweet marjoram) to go in tomato sauce for pasta.

Alternatively, and for something a little different, you could plant up a **hanging basket** with herbs. Plant *Mentha spicata* (mint), *Allium schoenoprasum* (chives), and *Salvia officinalis* Purpurascens Group (purple sage) in the top of the basket, with *Thymus pulegioides* (broad-leaved thyme) and *Fragaria vesca* (alpine strawberry) around the sides. After a time the mint would start to take over, but you could then transfer it to a pot or basket of its own.

Fragrant herbs

Some herbs are lovely grown solely for their fragrance.

• *Lavandula angustifolia* 'Hidcote' (lavender) with *Thymus citriodorus* 'Silver Queen' (lemon thyme), *Nepeta hybrida* 'Pink Candy' (catmint) and *Reseda odorata* (sweet mignonette) would make an attractive display.

• Or you could have a lemon-themed combination of *Aloysia triphylla* (lemon verbena), *Melissa officinalis* 'Aurea' (variegated lemon balm), *Thymus citriodorus* 'Golden Lemon' (golden lemon thyme) and *Monarda citriodora* (lemon bergamot).

Mentha spicata   *Rosmarinus officinalis*

A selection of Herbs for Containers

These are just a few suggestions. Try out some different groupings to suit your own space and style – as long as you choose bee-friendly plants, of course!

And Finally

I hope that by the time you read this you will be a little more confident about what sort of plants to put in your garden to attract and sustain bees, and how to arrange them in such a way that you find the end result attractive to look at – and that you will be inspired enough to put it into practice!

But now I will finish where I began, with my paraphrase of William Morris's quotation, and an appeal that you will:

Have no plant in your garden that you do not know to be useful to bees or believe to be beautiful.

Appendix 1
Plant Families and Species used in this Book

PRIMARY FAMILIES
Asteraceae
Achillea sp
Aster sp
Calendula sp
Callistephus sp
Centaurea sp
Chamaemelum sp
Cicorium sp
Cirsium sp
Coreopsis sp
Cosmos sp
Dahlia sp
Doronicum sp
Echinacea sp
Echinops sp
Gaillardia sp
Helenium sp
Helianthus sp
Liatris sp
Rudbeckia sp
Tanacetum sp

Lamiaceae
Agastache sp
Ajuga sp
Hyssopus sp
Lamium sp
Lavandula sp
Melissa sp

Mentha sp
Monarda sp
Nepeta sp
Ocimum sp
Origanum sp
Perovskia sp
Rosmarinus sp
Salvia sp
Satureja sp
Stachys sp
Teucrium sp
Thymus sp

SECONDARY
FAMILIES
Boraginaceae
Anchusa sp
Borago sp
Echium sp
Heliotropium sp
Lithodora sp
Myosotis sp
Pulmonaria sp

Ranunculaceae
Aconitum sp
Anemone sp
Clematis sp
Nigella sp
Thalictrum sp

Rosaceae
Cotoneaster sp
Fragaria sp
Geum sp
Malus sp
Prunus sp
Pyrus sp
Rosa sp

Scrophulariaceae
Digitalis sp
Hebe sp
Penstemon sp
Verbascum sp
Veronica sp

OTHER FAMILIES
Alliaceae
Allium sp

Apiaceae
Ammi sp
Astrantia sp
Daucus sp
Eryngium sp
Petroselinum sp

Araliaceae
Hedera sp

Asphodelaceae
Kniphofia sp
Ornithogalum sp

Berberidaceae
Mahonia sp

Brassicaceae
Erysimum sp
Iberis sp

Buddlejaceae
Buddleja sp

Campanulaceae
Campanula sp

Caprifoliaceae
Lonicera sp
Viburnum sp

Caryophyllaceae
Saponaria sp

Crassulaceae
Sedum sp

Dipsacaceae
Cephalaria sp
Knautia sp
Scabiosa sp

Ericaceae
Calluna sp
Enkianthus sp
Erica sp
Gaultheria sp

Kalmia sp
Vaccinium sp

Geraniaceae
Geranium sp

Hyacinthaceae
Camassia sp

Hydrangeaceae
Hydrangea sp

Hydrophyllaceae
Phacelia sp

Hypericaceae
Hypericum sp

Iridaceae
Crocus sp

Liliaceae
Agapanthus sp
Tulipa sp

Malvaceae
Alcea sp
Sidalcea sp

Myrtaceae
Leptospermum sp

Onagraceae
Clarkia sp

Papaveraceae
Papaver sp

Plumbaginaceae
Limonium sp

Polemoniaceae
Polemonium sp

Resedaceae
Reseda sp

Rutaceae
Skimmia sp

Salicaceae
Salix sp

Saxifragaceae
Heuchera sp

Thymelaeaceae
Daphne sp

Verbenaceae
Aloysia sp
Caryopteris sp
Verbena sp

Violaceae
Viola sp

Appendix 2
Table of Bee-friendly Plants

This table lists bee-friendly plants arranged according to the following order:

1. Plant families (Primary, Secondary, Other)
2. Function (focus, framework, flowers, fillers)
3. Season of flowering
4. Alphabetical order

Information is also given about the colour of the flower, whether or not the plant is evergreen, and the height and spread of each plant.

Abbreviations

Col	Colour of flower
B	Blue
C	Cream
G	Green
L	Lilac
M	Maroon
O	Orange
P	Purple
Pk	Pink
R	Red
V	Various
W	White
Y	Yellow

E/grn	Whether or not the plant is evergreen:
✗	no
✓	yes

✻	Season of flowering
Sp	Spring
Su	Summer
Au	Autumn

Ht   Approximate average height at maturity (bear in mind this may take many years to achieve)

Sprd Approximate average spread at maturity (bear in mind this may take many years to achieve)

	Col	E/grn	Sp	Su	Au	Ht	Sprd
PRIMARY							
Focus							
None							
Framework							
None							
Flowers							
Ajuga reptens 'Atropurpurea'	P	✓	✻			15cm	75cm
Doronicum 'Miss Mason'	Y	✗	✻			45cm	50cm
Doronicum x *excelsum* 'Harpur Crewe'	Y	✗	✻			60cm	50cm
Rosmarinus officinalis	B	✓	✻			1.2m	1m
Lamium maculatum 'Orchid Frost'	Pk	✓	✻	✻	✻	20cm	75cm
Achillea 'Credo'	Y	✗		✻		75cm	60cm
Achillea 'Marmalade'	O	✗		✻		75cm	60cm
Achillea 'Pretty Belinda'	Pk	✗		✻		75cm	60cm
Achillea ptarmica	W	✗		✻		75cm	60cm

	Col	E/grn	Sp	Su	Au	Ht	Sprd
Calendula officinalis	O	✗		✻		50cm	40cm
Chamaemelum nobile	W	✗		✻		30cm	45cm
Cirsium rivulare 'Atropurpureum'	M	✗		✻		1.2m	60cm
Coreopsis 'Limerock Passion'	R	✗		✻		45cm	50cm
Echinops ritro 'Veitch's Blue'	B	✗		✻		1.2m	75cm
Gaillardia 'Oranges and Lemons'	O	✗		✻		60cm	50cm
Hyssopus officinalis	B	✓		✻		45cm	45cm
Lavandula angustifolia 'Hidcote'	P	✓		✻		60cm	75cm
Melissa officinalis 'Aurea'	C	✗		✻		50cm	45cm
Melissa sp	C	✗		✻		50cm	45cm
Mentha sp	P/W	✗		✻		45cm	indef
Mentha spicata	P	✗		✻		45cm	indef
Mentha spicata var. *crispa* 'Moroccan'	W	✗		✻		45cm	indef
Monarda 'Aquarius'	P/Pk	✗		✻		90cm	45cm
Monarda didyma 'Gardenview Scarlet'	R	✗		✻		90cm	45cm
Monarda fistulosa	P	✗		✻		1m	45cm
Origanum laevigatum 'Herrenhausen'	M	✓		✻		45cm	45cm
Origanum vulgare	W	✗		✻		45cm	45cm
Salvia officinalis	P	✓		✻		75cm	50cm
Salvia officinalis Purpurascens Group	P	✓		✻		60cm	50cm
Salvia x *sylvestris* 'Blauhügel'	P	✗		✻		60cm	45cm
Satureja montana	W	✓		✻		30cm	20cm
Stachys byzantina	Pk	✗		✻		30cm	50cm
Teucrium x *lucidrys*	Pk	✓		✻		25cm	30cm
Thymus 'Jekka'	Pk	✓		✻		25cm	30cm
Thymus citriodorus 'Golden Lemon'	Pk	✓		✻		20cm	30cm

	Col	E/grn	Sp	Su	Au	Ht	Sprd
Thymus citriodorus 'Silver Queen'	Pk	✓		❀		20cm	30cm
Thymus pulegioides	Pk	✓		❀		20cm	30cm
Thymus vulgaris	Pk	✓		❀		20cm	30cm
Thymus vulgaris 'Compactus'	Pk	✓		❀		20cm	20cm
Achillea 'Apfelblüte'	Pk	✗		❀	❀	75cm	60cm
Achillea 'Lilac Beauty'	L	✗		❀	❀	75cm	60cm
Achillea 'Martina'	Y	✗		❀	❀	75cm	60cm
Achillea 'Terracotta'	O	✗		❀	❀	75cm	60cm
Agastache 'Black Adder'	P	✗		❀	❀	90cm	40cm
Centaurea scabiosa	B	✗		❀	❀	90cm	45cm
Cicorium intybus	B	✗		❀	❀	1.2m	60cm
Echinacea purpurea 'Primadonna White'	W	✗		❀	❀	90cm	50cm
Echinacea purpurea 'White Swan'	W	✗		❀	❀	90cm	50cm
Echinops bannaticus 'Blue Pearl'	B	✗		❀	❀	1.2m	60cm
Helenium 'Gartensonne'	Y	✗		❀	❀	90cm	60cm
Helenium 'Kanaria'	Y	✗		❀	❀	90cm	60cm
Helenium 'Moerheim Beauty'	O	✗		❀	❀	90cm	60cm
Helenium 'Waltraut'	O	✗		❀	❀	90cm	60cm
Liatris spicata	P/Pk	✗		❀	❀	60cm	30cm
Nepeta hybrida 'Pink Candy'	Pk	✗		❀	❀	60cm	50cm
Nepeta racemosa 'Walker's Low'	B	✗		❀	❀	60cm	50cm
Perovskia atriplicifolia 'Little Spire'	B	✗		❀	❀	60cm	60cm
Salvia nemerosa 'Amethyst'	P	✗		❀	❀	60cm	45cm
Aster divaricatus	W	✗			❀	75cm	45cm
Aster novi-belgii 'Dandy'	Pk	✗			❀	45cm	45cm
Aster x *frikartii* 'Mönch'	P	✗			❀	75cm	45cm
Dahlia 'Bishop of Llandaff'	R	✗			❀	75cm	45cm

	Col	E/grn	Sp	Su	Au	Ht	Sprd
Dahlia 'Bishop of York'	Y	✗			❋	75cm	45cm
Dahlia 'Mermaid of Zennor'	L/Pk	✗			❋	75cm	50cm
Dahlia 'Moonfire'	Y/O	✗			❋	75cm	45cm
Dahlia 'Romeo'	R	✗			❋	50cm	45cm
Dahlia sp	V	✗			❋	75cm	50cm
Echinacea purpurea	Pk/P	✗			❋	90cm	50cm
Echinacea purpurea 'Harvest Moon'	Y	✗			❋	90cm	50cm
Echinacea purpurea 'Pow Wow'	Pk/P	✗			❋	90cm	50cm
Echinacea purpurea 'Sunrise'	Y	✗			❋	90cm	50cm
Rudbeckia hirta 'Prairie Sun'	Y	✗			❋	75cm	50cm
Fillers							
Callistephus chinensis	V	✗		❋		45cm	30cm
Centaurea cyanus	B	✗		❋		50cm	15cm
Fragaria vesca	W	✓		❋		30cm	20cm
Monarda citriodora	P/Pk	✗		❋		30cm	30cm
Ocimum basilicum	W	✗		❋		45cm	30cm
Origanum majorana	W	✗		❋		30cm	30cm
Amberboa moschata	V	✗		❋	❋	45cm	20cm
Cosmos bipinnatus	W/Pk	✗		❋	❋	90cm	40cm
Helianthus annuus 'Garden Statement'	Y	✗		❋	❋	80cm	30cm

SECONDARY

Focus

	Col	E/grn	Sp	Su	Au	Ht	Sprd
Crataegus monogyna	W	✗	❋			8m	5m
Cydonia oblonga	Pk/W	✗	❋			5m	5m
Malus sp	W	✗	❋			6m	5m
Mespilus germanica	W	✗	❋			8m	6m
Prunus sp	Pk/W	✗	❋			8m	6m

	Col	E/grn	Sp	Su	Au	Ht	Sprd
Pyrus sp	W	✗	❀			8m	6m
Sorbus aucuparia	W	✗	❀			10m	7m

Framework

	Col	E/grn	Sp	Su	Au	Ht	Sprd
Clematis 'Elsa Spath'	L	✗	❀			2.5m	50cm
Prunus laurocerasus 'Otto Luyken'	W	✓	❀			75cm	1.5m
Ribes sp	V	✗	❀			1.5m	1m
Rubus sp	Pk/W	✗	❀			1.5m	2m
Clematis montana 'Crinkle'	Pk/P	✗	❀	❀		5m	1m
Cotoneaster harrovianus	W	✓		❀		1.5m	1m
Cotoneaster microphyllus	W	✓		❀		1m	1.5m
Rosa 'Nutkana'	Pk	✗		❀		1.5m	1m
Rosa gallica var. *officinalis*	Pk	✗		❀		1.2m	1.2m
Clematis 'Etoile Violette'	P	✗		❀	❀	3m	1.2m
Hebe 'Autumn Glory'	P	✓		❀	❀	60cm	75cm
Rosa 'Jaquenetta'	O	✗		❀	❀	1.5m	1.2m
Rosa 'Kew Gardens'	W	✗		❀	❀	1.5m	1m
Rosa 'Rose of Picardy'	R	✗		❀	❀	1.2m	1m
Rosa 'Scintillation'	Pk	✗		❀	❀	1.2m	1.5m
Rosa 'Windrush'	Y	✗		❀	❀	1.2m	1.2m

Flowers

	Col	E/grn	Sp	Su	Au	Ht	Sprd
Pulmonaria 'Beth's Pink'	P	✗	❀			20cm	20cm
Pulmonaria 'Cotton Cool'	B/P	✓	❀			20cm	20cm
Pulmonaria angustifolia 'Mawson's Variety'	B	✗	❀			20cm	20cm
Anchusa azurea 'Loddon Royalist'	B	✗	❀	❀		1m	60cm

	Col	E/grn	Sp	Su	Au	Ht	Sprd
Myosotis sp	B	✗	❊	❊		20cm	15cm
Digitalis grandiflora	Y	✓		❊		90cm	50cm
Digitalis purpurea	Pk/P	✗		❊		90cm	50cm
Digitalis purpurea 'Pam's Choice'	W/P	✗		❊		90cm	50cm
Lithodora diffusa 'Heavenly Blue'	B	✓		❊		15cm	50cm
Penstemon 'Blackberry Fancy'	M	✗		❊		75cm	45cm
Penstemon 'Blackberry Fudge'	M	✗		❊		75cm	45cm
Penstemon 'Vanilla Plum'	R	✗		❊		75cm	45cm
Thalictrum lucidum	Y	✗		❊		1m	50cm
Verbascum 'Cherry Helen'	Pk	✗		❊		75cm	30cm
Verbascum 'Gainsborough'	Y	✗		❊		75cm	30cm
Verbascum 'Sierra Sunset'	Y	✗		❊		75cm	30cm
Penstemon 'Tubular Bells Pink'	Pk	✗		❊	❊	60cm	45cm
Verbascum nigrum	W	✗		❊	❊	75cm	30cm
Veronica longifolia	P	✗		❊	❊	1m	50cm
Veronica longifolia 'Blue John'	B/P	✗		❊	❊	1m	50cm
Veronica longifolia 'Romily Purple'	P	✗		❊	❊	1m	50cm
Aconitum carmichaelii Wilsonii Group	B/P	✗			❊	1m	45cm
Aconitum car michaelii Wilsonii Group 'Spaetlese'	B	✗			❊	1m	45cm

Fillers

	Col	E/grn	Sp	Su	Au	Ht	Sprd
Anemone blanda	V	✗	❊			5cm	10cm
Anemone nemerosa 'Alba'	W	✗	❊			15cm	30cm
Anemone nemerosa 'Allenii'	B	✗	❊			15cm	30cm
Anemone nemerosa 'Pentre Pink'	Pk	✗	❊			15cm	30cm
Eranthis hyemalis	Y	✗	❊			10cm	10cm

	Col	E/grn	Sp	Su	Au	Ht	Sprd
Borago officinalis	B	✗		❋		50cm	50cm
Echium 'Blue Bedder'	B	✗		❋		30cm	30cm
Nigella damascena	B	✗		❋		60cm	20cm
Heliotropium arborescens	P	✗		❋	❋	45cm	30cm

OTHER

Focus

	Col	E/grn	Sp	Su	Au	Ht	Sprd
Aesculus hippocastanum	W	✗	❋			15m	12m
Corylus avellana	Y	✗	❋			6m	5m
Ilex aquifolium	W	✓	❋			15m	6m
Salix caprea	W	✗	❋			10m	8m
Salix hastata 'Wehrhahnii'	W	✗	❋			1.5m	1.5m
Castanea sativa	W	✗		❋		30m	15m
Catalpa bignonioides	W	✗		❋		15m	15m
Sophora japonica	W	✗		❋		20m	20m
Tetradium daniellii	W	✗		❋		15m	15m
Tilia sp	Y	✗		❋		30m	15m

Framework

	Col	E/grn	Sp	Su	Au	Ht	Sprd
Daphne mezereum	Pk	✗	❋			1.5m	1m
Daphne tangutica	W	✓	❋			1.5m	1.5m
Enkianthus campanulatus 'Pagoda Bush'	W	✗	❋			2m	1.5m
Laurus nobilis	Y	✓	❋			10m	5m
Mahonia aquifolium	Y	✓	❋			1m	1.5m
Philadelphus sp	W	✗	❋			2m	2m
Skimmia x *confusa* 'Kew Green'	G	✓	❋			75cm	75cm

	Col	E/grn	Sp	Su	Au	Ht	Sprd
Viburnum tinus 'Eve Price'	W	✓	✽			1.5m	1.5m
Viburnum x *bodnantense*	Pk	✗	✽			3m	3m
Gaultheria x *wisleyensis* 'Wisley Pearl'	W	✓	✽	✽		1.5m	1.5m
Leptospermum scoparium	W	✓	✽	✽		1.5m	1.5m
Vaccinium corymbosum	W	✗	✽	✽		1.5m	1m
Ulex europaeus	Y	✓	✽	✽	✽	75cm	75cm
Kalmia latifolia	Pk	✓		✽		3m	3m
Lonicera x *tellmanniana*	O	✗		✽		4m	50cm
Buddleja davidii 'Empire Blue'	P	✗		✽	✽	4m	3m
Buddleja x *weyeriana* 'Sungold'	Y	✗		✽	✽	3m	3m
Caryopteris x *clandonensis* 'Grand Bleu'	B	✗		✽	✽	1m	1m
Caryopteris x *clandonensis* 'Worcester Gold'	B	✗		✽	✽	1m	1m
Eucryphia x *nymansensis* 'Nymansay'	W	✓		✽	✽	12m	7m
Hydrangea aspera subsp *sargentiana*	P/W	✗		✽	✽	3m	3m
Hypericum 'Hidcote'	Y	✓		✽	✽	1.2m	2m
Hedera sp	W	✓			✽	10m	5m

Flowers

	Col	E/grn	Sp	Su	Au	Ht	Sprd
Erica x *darleyensis* 'Darley Dale'	M	✓	✽			50cm	50cm

	Col	E/grn	Sp	Su	Au	Ht	Sprd
Erysimum 'Winter Sorbet'	V	✓	❀			50cm	40cm
Erica x *darleyensis* 'White Glow'	W	✓	❀	❀		50cm	50cm
Geranium macrorrhizum 'Ingwersen's Variety'	P	✓	❀	❀		30cm	50cm
Geranium macrorrhizum 'Mt Olympus White'	W	✓	❀	❀		30cm	50cm
Iris germanica 'Florentina'	W	✓	❀	❀		1m	50cm
Viola tricolor	V	✗	❀	❀	❀	10cm	10cm
Alcea ficifolia	W	✗		❀		1m	45cm
Aloysia triphylla	W	✗		❀		60cm	50cm
Ammi majus	W	✗		❀		75cm	20cm
Astrantia major 'Moulin Rouge'	M	✗		❀		60cm	45cm
Astrantia major 'Venice'	M	✗		❀		60cm	45cm
Campanula glomerata	P	✗		❀		75cm	50cm
Centranthus ruber	Pk	✗		❀		60cm	45cm
Daucus carota	W	✗		❀		20cm	10cm
Eryngium bourgatii 'Picos Amethyst'	B	✗		❀		60cm	45cm
Eryngium x *tripartitum* 'Jade Frost'	B	✗		❀		60cm	45cm
Geranium 'Kashmir Pink'	Pk	✗		❀		45cm	45cm
Geranium 'Patricia'	P	✗		❀		45cm	45cm
Geranium pratense	P	✗		❀		45cm	45cm
Geranium x *oxonianum* 'Claridge Druce'	Pk	✗		❀		45cm	45cm

	Col	E/grn	Sp	Su	Au	Ht	Sprd
Heuchera 'Beaujolais'	W	✓		❋		45cm	45cm
Heuchera 'Bressingham Bronze'	W	✓		❋		30cm	25cm
Limonium binervosum	B	✗		❋		75cm	40cm
Papaver orientale 'Beauty of Livermere'	R	✗		❋		80cm	60cm
Papaver orientale 'Bolero'	Pk/P	✗		❋		80cm	60cm
Papaver orientale 'Patty's Plum'	Pk/P	✗		❋		80cm	60cm
Petroselinum crispum	W	✓		❋		30cm	15cm
Polemonium caeruleum	P	✗		❋		50cm	45cm
Saponaria officinalis	Pk	✗		❋		60cm	60cm
Scabiosa caucasica 'Clive Greaves'	B	✗		❋		45cm	45cm
Scabiosa columbaria	L/B	✗		❋		75cm	30cm
Sidalcea 'Elsie Heugh'	Pk	✗		❋		90cm	60cm
Sidalcea 'Sussex Beauty'	Pk	✗		❋		90cm	60cm
Calluna vulgaris 'Red Pimpernel'	Pk	✓		❋	❋	30cm	30cm
Calluna vulgaris 'Silver Queen'	Pk	✓		❋	❋	30cm	30cm
Campanula lactiflora 'Prichard's Variety'	P	✗		❋	❋	75cm	60cm
Geranium pratense var. *striatum* 'Splish Splash'	W/P	✗		❋	❋	45cm	45cm
Geranium sanguineum 'Elke'	Pk	✗		❋	❋	45cm	45cm
Kniphofia 'Bees' Sunset'	Y	✗		❋	❋	90cm	50cm
Kniphofia 'Bressingham Comet'	O	✗		❋	❋	45cm	30cm

	Col	E/grn	Sp	Su	Au	Ht	Sprd
Kniphofia 'Ice Queen'	C	✗		❋	❋	75cm	45cm
Kniphofia 'Toffee Nosed'	O/Y	✗		❋	❋	90cm	50cm
Polemonium 'Bressingham Purple' P		✗		❋	❋	50cm	45cm
Scabiosa columbaria subsp *ochroleuca* 'Moon Dance'	Y	✗		❋	❋	90cm	60cm
Sedum 'Brilliant'	Pk	✗			❋	45cm	45cm
Sedum 'Strawberries and Cream'	M/Pk	✗			❋	45cm	45cm

Fillers

	Col	E/grn	Sp	Su	Au	Ht	Sprd
Allium multibulbosum	W	✗	❋			60cm	5cm
Camassia leichtlinii	B	✗	❋			90cm	20cm
Crocus sp	V	✗	❋			5cm	4cm
Erysimum cheiri	V	✓	❋			30cm	25cm
Muscari sp	B	✗	❋			15cm	8cm
Tulipa sp	V	✗	❋			30cm	15cm
Allium 'Purple Sensation'	P	✗		❋		60cm	5cm
Allium ampeloprasum	W	✗		❋		1m	5cm
Allium caeruleum	B	✗		❋		60cm	5cm
Allium neapolitanum Cowanii Group	W	✗		❋		30cm	5cm
Allium sphaerocephalon	M	✗		❋		60cm	5cm
Clarkia elegans	V	✗		❋		60cm	30cm
Eschscholzia californica	O/Y	✗		❋		30cm	15cm
Iberis umbellate	V	✗		❋		20cm	20cm
Ornithogalum pyrenaicum	W	✗		❋		20cm	10cm
Papaver somniferum	V	✗		❋		60cm	30cm
Phacelia tanacetifolia	B	✗		❋		60cm	30cm
Reseda odorata	Y	✗		❋		40cm	30cm

	Col	E/grn	Sp	Su	Au	Ht	Sprd
Allium schoenoprasum	Pk	✗		❀	❀	25cm	5cm
Limnanthes douglasii	W/Y	✗		❀	❀	15cm	10cm
Verbena bonariensis	P	✗		❀	❀	1.2m	60cm
Verbena rigida	P	✗		❀	❀	50cm	30cm
Colchicum autumnale	Pk/P	✗			❀	10cm	10cm

Further Reading

Brickell, C. (ed.) (2010) *The Royal Horticultural Society Encyclopedia of Plants and Flowers*, 5th edition. Dorling Kindersley.

Brooks, John (2001) *Garden Design*. Dorling Kindersley.

Cramp, D. (2008) *A Practical Manual of Beekeeping*. Spring Hill.

Howes, F.N. (1945) *Plants and Beekeeping*. Faber & Faber. Available as download from www.archive.org.

Hughes, Craig (2010) *Urban Beekeeping*. The Good Life Press.

International Bee Research Association (2008) *Garden Plants Valuable to Bees*. IBRA.

Leach, Helen (2000) *Cultivating Myths: Fiction, Fact and Fashion in Garden History*. Random House New Zealand.

Little, Maureen (2011) *The Bee Garden*. Spring Hill.

McVicar, J. (2009) *Jekka's Complete Herb Book*. Kyle Cathie.

Mountain, M.F. (1965) *Trees and Shrubs Valuable to Bees*. International Bee Research Association.

Royal Horticultural Society (2010) *Royal Horticultural Society Entomology Advisory Leaflet No 6204*.

Useful Addresses and Websites

The Bee Garden
1 Hereford Grove
Cottam
Preston
Lancashire PR4 0NS
www.thebeegarden.co.uk
Useful information about all aspects of gardening for bees.

Plant related

Royal Horticultural Society
80 Vincent Square
London SW1P 2PE
www.rhs.org.uk

Garden Organic
Coventry
Warwickshire CV8 3LG
www.gardenorganic.org.uk

The Garden Studio
151a Southport New Road
Tarleton
Preston
Lancashire PR4 6HX
Contact Tricia Brown: 01772 812672
Specialist perennial nursery, open to the public.

Jekka's Herb Farm
Rose Cottage
Shellards Lane
Alveston
Bristol BS35 3SY
www.jekkasherbfarm.com
Organic herb grower. Mail order and online sales.

Cotswold Garden Flowers
Sands Lane
Badsey
Worcestershire WR11 7EZ
www.cgf.net
Specialist nursery, open to the public and mail order.

Keepers Nursery
Gallants Court
East Farleigh
Maidstone
Kent ME15 0LE
www.keepers-nursery.co.uk
Supplier of fruit trees.

National Fruit Collection
www.brogdaleonline.co.uk
Useful information on all sorts of fruit.

David Austin Roses
Bowling Green Lane
Albrighton
Wolverhampton WV7 3HB
www.davidaustinroses.com
Supplier of roses of all descriptions.

Natural History Museum
Cromwell Road
London SW7 5BD
www.nhm.ac.uk/nature-online/life/plants-fungi/postcode-plants
Free online database of what wild flowers can be found in your locality.

Bee related

Crossmoor Honey Farm
Keeps Barn Farm
Crossmoor
Preston
Lancashire PR4 3XB
www.crossmoorhoney.com
Beekeeping courses, hive equipment, honey and lots of information about honeybees.

International Bee Research Association (IBRA)
18 North Road
Cardiff CF1 3DY
www.ibra.org.uk
A not-for-profit organization that aims to increase awareness of the vital role of bees in the environment.

British Beekeepers' Association
National Beekeeping Centre
National Agricultural Centre
Stoneleigh
Warwickshire CV8 2LZ
www.britishbee.org.uk

Bumblebee Conservation Trust
School of Biological & Environmental Sciences
University of Stirling
Stirling FK9 4LA
www.bumblebeeconservation.org.uk

Index of Illustrated Plants

List of Common Names of Plants and their Latin Equivalents

Alpine strawberry	*Fragaria vesca*
Apple	*Malus domestica*
Basil	*Ocimum*
Bay	*Laurus nobilis*
Bee balm	*Monarda*
Bellflower	*Campanula*
Bergamot	*Monarda*
Black currant	*Ribes nigrum*
Blackberry	*Rubus fruticosus*
Black-eyed Susan	*Rudbeckia*
Borage	*Borago officinalis*
Bugle	*Ajuga*
Butterfly bush	*Buddleja*
Candytuft	*Iberis umbellata*
Catmint	*Nepeta*
Cherry pie plant	*Heliotropium*
Chicory	*Cicorium intybus*
China aster	*Callistephus chinensis*
Chives	*Allium schoenoprasum*
Comfrey	*Symphytum officinale*
Coneflower	*Echinacea*
Coneflower	*Rudbeckia*
Cornflower	*Centaurea cyanus*
Crab apple	*Malus sylvestris*
Cranesbill	*Geranium*
Dandelion	*Taraxacum officinale*
Deadnettle	*Lamium maculatum*
Dogrose	*Rosa canina*
Field scabious	*Knautia arvensis*

Foxglove	*Digitalis*
Giant hyssop	*Agastache*
Globe thistle	*Echinops*
Gorse	*Ulex europaeus*
Grape hyacinth	*Muscari*
Hawthorn	*Crataegus monogyna*
Heartsease	*Viola tricolor*
Heather	*Erica, Calluna*
Heliotrope	*Heliotropium*
Honeysuckle	*Lonicera*
Hyssop	*Hyssopus officinalis*
Ice plant	*Sedum*
Ivy	*Hedera*
Jacob's ladder	*Polemonium*
Knapweed	*Centaurea scabiosa*
Lamb's ears	*Stachys byzantina*
Lavender	*Lavandula*
Lemon Balm	*Melissa officinalis*
Lemon Verbena	*Aloysia triphylla*
Leopard's Bane	*Doronicum*
Love-in-a-mist	*Nigella*
Lungwort	*Pulmonaria*
Manuka	*Leptospermum scoparium*
Marjoram	*Origanum*
Masterwort	*Astrantia*
May	*Crataegus monogyna*
Meadow cranesbill	*Geranium pratense*
Meadow geranium	*Geranium pratense*
Michaelmas daisies	*Aster novi-belgii* and *A. novae-angliae*
Mint	*Mentha*
Monkshood	*Aconitum*
Old Man's Beard	*Clematis vitalba*
Oregon grape	*Mahonia aquifolium*
Oriental poppy	*Papaver orientale*
Ornamental onion	*Allium*
Pear	*Pyrus communis*
Pot marigold	*Calendula officinalis*

Quickthorn	*Crataegus monogyna*
Raspberry	*Rubus idaeus*
Red currant	*Ribes rubrum*
Red deadnettle	*Lamium purpureum*
Red hot poker	*Kniphofia*
Rose	*Rosa*
Rosemary	*Rosmarinus officinalis*
Russian comfrey	*Symphytum* x *uplandicum*
Russian sage	*Perovskia atriplicifolia*
Sage	*Salvia*
Sea holly	*Eryngium*
Sloe	*Prunus spinosa*
Small scabious	*Scabiosa columbaria*
Sneezeweed	*Helenium*
Soapwort	*Saponaria officinalis*
Sunflower	*Helianthus annuus*
Sweet sultan	*Amberboa moschata*
Tea tree	*Leptospermum scoparium*
Thyme	*Thymus*
Viper's bugloss	*Echium vulgare*
Wall germander	*Teucrium* x *lucidrys*
Wallflower	*Erysimum*
Wild carrot	*Daucus carota*
Wild mignonette	*Reseda lutea*
Windflower	*Anemone blanda*
Winter aconite	*Eranthis hyemalis*
Winter savory	*Satureja montana*
Wolfsbane	*Aconitum*
Yarrow	*Achillea*

Index of Plants

Index

Bee-friendly plants   ix, x, xi, 1, 3, 5, 15, 20–9, 30, 31, 36, 68, 94, 100, 116, 126, 140, 150, 162
Bee hives 19
Beekeeper's garden 33, 158–61

Colour 8, 9, 10, 14, 15, 20, 23–5, 33
    wheel 11, 24
Containers 7, 162–73

Design
    balance in 8, 9, 13, 15, 62
    colour in 8, 9, 10
    elements 8, 10–13
    focalization in 8, 9, 62
    form in 8, 9, 10, 11, 14, 16, 62
    line in 8, 9, 11–13
    movement in 8, 9, 11, 14, 15
    plants in 13–17
    principles 8, 9–10
    proportion in 8, 9, 12, 13, 14
    repetition in 8, 9–10, 15, 62
    scale in 8, 10, 12
    texture in 8, 9, 10, 12, 14, 27, 62
    time in 13

Fence(s) 5, 6–7, 20, 106
Fibonacci 134
Food
    for bees ix, x, 6, 15, 19, 20, 21, 26

Garden
    aspect of 1, 31
    conditions 1–7, 31, 33
Golden Ratio 62

Habitats for bees ix, 6, 19
Hanging basket(s) 172
Hedge(s) 5–6, 56, 120, 140, 159

June Gap 26